The Journey in Between

Navigating the Terrain in Between Life's Moments

Eileen Deadwiler

DALLAS, TEXAS

All rights reserved. No part of this book may be reproduced or transmitted in any form or by any means, electronic or mechanical, including photocopying, recording, or by any information storage and retrieval system, without permission in writing from the copyright owner. The views expressed in this work are solely those of the author and do not necessarily reflect the views of the publisher, and the publisher hereby disclaims any responsibility for them.

THE HOLY BIBLE, NEW INTERNATIONAL VERSION®, NIV® Copyright © 1973, 1978, 1984, 2011 by Biblica, Inc.™ Used by permission. All rights reserved worldwide.

Scripture quotations taken from the Amplified® Bible (AMP), Copyright © 2015 by The Lockman Foundation Used by permission. www.Lockman.org.

Scripture quotations taken from the (NASB®) New American Standard Bible®, Copyright © 1960, 1971, 1977, 1995, 2020 by The Lockman Foundation.
Used by permission. All rights reserved. Lockman.org.

Scripture taken from the New King James Version®. Copyright © 1982 by Thomas Nelson, Inc. Used by permission. All rights reserved. Unless otherwise noted.

Copyright © 2022 * Higgins Publishing. All rights reserved.
Eileen Deadwiler * The Journey in Between: *Navigating the Terrain in Between Life's Moments*

Higgins Publishing supports the rights to free expression and the value of copyright. The purpose of copyright is to encourage writers and artists to produce creative works that enrich our values. The scanning, uploading, and distribution of this book without the express permission of the publisher is a theft of intellectual property. If you would like permission to use material from this book (other than for review purposes), please contact permissions@higginspublishing.com. Thank you for your support of copyright law.

Higgins Publishing | www.higginspublishing.com - The publisher is not responsible for websites (or their content) that are not owned by the publisher. Higgins Publishing is committed to excellence in the publishing industry. The company reflects the philosophy established by the founder, based on Psalm 68:11, 'The Lord gave the word, and great was the company of those who published it.'

Library of Congress Control Number: 20229017802
pcm 140 – Includes Index * Appendix.   May 2023

Deadwiler, Eileen * The Journey in Between: *Navigating the Terrain in Between Life's Moments*

ISBN: 978-1-941580-22-6 (PB) * 978-1-941580-23-3 (HB) * 978-1-941580-18-9 (EB)
REL012000   RELIGION / Christian Living / General
REL011000   RELIGION / Christian Education / General
REL012120   RELIGION / Christian Living / Spiritual Growth

Table of Contents

Dedication vii

Foreword ix

Introduction xi

Chapter 1: What is the Journey In Between? 1
    Appointed Times 2
    Accounting for the Past 5

Chapter 2: Navigating the Plains 7
    The Navigator 8
    The Plains 10

Chapter 3: Testing in the Wilderness 15
    All that Is in the World 16
    Lust of the Flesh 17
    Jesus' Response 1 19
    Lust of the Eyes 20
    Jesus' Response 2 22
    Pride of Life 23
    Jesus' Response 3 25

Chapter 4: Into the Jungle 27
    It's Like a Jungle 28
    Surviving the Jungle 34

Chapter 5: Guerilla Warfare in the Jungle 37
    Warfare in the Jungle 38

    The Armor 42

Chapter 6: Rivers in the Desert 53

    The Desert 54

Chapter 7: An Encounter in the Valley 63

    Weeping for a Night 64

    The Valley 66

    Pausing Isn't Pretty 67

    Embrace The Pause 68

Chapter 8: Lily of the Valley 71

    The Gospel According to Dexter 72

    Lily of the Valley 73

    An Encounter with the Lily (Jesus) 74

    True Worship 76

Chapter 9: Mountain to Mountain Top 79

    For Purple Mountains Majesty 80

    The Climb 81

    Take A Hike 82

    Discipline 84

    Plan Your Campaign – Plan Your Consecration 85

    Acclimatize – Set Your Environment 88

    Travel Light – Clear Your Mind 89

    Watch Out for Weather: Know the Climate 91

    Get Down Alive – a Posture of Humility 93

Chapter 10: Rough Road Ahead 97
    Under Construction 98
    Grief – A Rough Road to Travel 100
    Marriage Journey 102
    Rough Road of Rejection 105
    The Excavation 107
Chapter 11: Celebrating Milestones 113
    A Time to Celebrate 114
About the Author 117
Index 119
Appendix 125

Dedication

I dedicate this labor of love to the following:

My Zoom Bible study ladies, for allowing me to share my heart and teach the lessons that eventually became chapters for this book.

My mother, for teaching me how to pray and leading me to the Lord on our living room couch when I was nine.

My children, Drew, Camille, Elise, Marquise, and Darren, for giving me moral support and words of encouragement that they truly believed in me to accomplish this.

Of course, my husband Derrick for loving, supporting, comforting, and challenging me to complete this passion project. I could not have done this without you, Babe.

And to My Lord and Savior Jesus Christ for enabling me to see this through!

FOREWORD

Nature tells us that transition seasons are part of the rhythm of life. Genesis 8:22 says, "While the earth remains, seedtime and harvest, cold and heat, winter and summer, and day and night shall not cease." Webster defines "transition" as "passage from one position, or state to another." But that transition period may be uncomfortable, even distressing, and Eileen's book begs the question: are we going to end up better or bitter? Those in between seasons can be some of the most challenging times of one's life. In my experience, in the natural, going from a well-paying construction job in California, to Bible school in Oklahoma at the age of 35, with a wife, a two-year-old, and a baby on the way, seemed crazy! We left our home, family, friends, and a secure job to move to Tulsa, Broken Arrow, Oklahoma, with no job, and very little money. It was a major test for me and my wife, trusting we were in the will of God, even though it was extremely difficult. This book by Eileen is written to encourage the reader to never give up even in the darkest of seasons. The key thing is to never get trapped in transition. God does not want us to live in the land of regret, pain, and disappointment. This book is to remind us that God wants us better, not bitter. It has been a joy to know Eileen and her husband Derrick over the years, two wonderful, gifted people I call friends.

Pastor Dick Bernal
Jubilee Legacy International

Introduction

I decided to write the book I wanted to read. Well, more like the book I needed to read.

Over the past few years, I have been searching for help and suggestions to help me find my "next." With search engines like Google, and literally millions of how-to YouTube videos out there in cyberspace, you can learn how to make anything, do anything, and be anything. Yet still, I could not find what I was looking for.

While I am writing this, the state of the world is in a global pandemic due to the COVID-19 virus. Not only has it taken the lives of millions around the world, it has reset our culture with new terms like "social distancing," "self-quarantine," and "shelter in place." The interesting part for me in this new world, is that I had already been in my own personal state of quarantine for a year and a half B.C. (Before COVID-19, for those playing along at home),

In 2018, I lost my self-defined dream job. In that same year, we moved from the beautiful Bay Area in Northern California to always sunny and sometimes hot (understatement) Las Vegas, Nevada. During that transition I struggled to find employment, a church, and a real community to connect with.

Operating in this limbo for the last several years has allowed me time to explore how I'd like to proceed with this next phase of my life. But then what does that even mean?

I am writing this in hopes of blessing and encouraging those who are looking for that "thing" that you can't Google or watch a video to learn. I am hoping to reach those who are in their "mid-life" and are now suddenly discovering that they have to start over in their career. You had your dream job and dream home, then all of sudden they're gone!

Introduction

Just as important, I am hoping to reach those who are grieving the death of a sibling, a parent, or a best friend. Or maybe grieving the loss of all three, as I have. I am hoping to relate to parents whose child is ill and needing surgery during a global pandemic.

In all this, I am hoping to share nuggets, scriptures, and spiritual insight into how God is truly good and how we can acknowledge His presence in everything. Even the in between times.

There are countless books, videos, sermons, TED talks and TikToks on what to do when we're in the inevitable valleys of life. And we never need any encouragement to brag about those triumphant, victorious mountain-top moments. So much bread was baked during lockdown, there was actually a shortage on yeast, people. We – America, the land of plenty – actually ran out of yeast because so many people were winning at baking bread. Seriously. Look up the hashtag #breadbaking.

In essence, I'm here to talk about those in between moments. Those are moments along this road of life that no one seems to really be talking about, the times when you're done with one phase of your life – either out of choice or necessity – though you haven't a single clue as to what your next step will be. Those times when you're looking back at your old successes, but new opportunities are mere shadows in a hazy fog.

I'm here to talk about the Journey In Between.

Chapter 1
What is the Journey In Between?

APPOINTED TIMES

A time to give birth and a time to die … (Ecclesiastes 3:2 NASB)

The journey in between can be about a large number of things: in between relationships, in between jobs, in between careers, in between churches, in between marriages, in between homes, in between now and your "next." Basically they're in between life events, milestones or transition points. The major journey in between is the long dash on your tombstone: what you did and how you lived from the sunrise of your birth to the sunset of your death. I know that can sound a bit morbid, but please bear with me.

The good news is, in Christ the long dashes are on the outside and your life is in between them. Our life started before we existed physically, and it will continue throughout eternity.

Before I formed you in the womb I knew you;
Before you were born I consecrated you … (Jeremiah 1:5 NASB)

In the meantime, we are just trying to live that dash as best we can here on earth. How we navigate the terrain in between the moments is what this journey is about. We will explore the experiences by applying the Word of God and hearing the voice of God on our way through five kinds of landscapes: the plains, the jungle, the desert, the valley, and even the mountaintop moments. This is an exciting adventure with lessons to learn and perspectives to explore.

What is the Journey in Between?

The Journey in Between is understanding that there is an appointed time for everything, a time for every event under heaven. Walking out this journey in this current time is no exception.

A time to give birth and a time to die;
A time to plant and a time to uproot what is planted.
A time to kill and a time to heal;

A time to tear down and a time to build up.
A time to weep and a time to laugh;

A time to mourn and a time to dance.
A time to throw stones and a time to gather stones;

A time to embrace and a time to shun embracing.
A time to search and a time to give up as lost;

A time to keep and a time to throw away.
A time to tear apart and a time to sew together;

A time to be silent and a time to speak.

A time to love and a time to hate; A time for war and a time for peace (Ecclesiastes 3:2-8 NASB, 2000).

Time can be defined as "the duration in which all things happen, or a precise instant that something happens."[1] We can also add, it is a measure of the state, situation, or actuality in

---

[1] YourDictionary, "Time (n)", accessed January 10, 2021, https://www.yourdictionary.com/time

which something happens. God created time and He ultimately controls what it is and how we, as His creation, move through it. Time is an aspect of God's divinity. For all creation, time didn't begin until Genesis 1:1, "In the beginning, God created…" because God was there before the beginning. God controls time and God sovereignly observes all of life's activities.

When reading the passage above you can exchange the word "time" with "divinely appointed" or God's appointed time. It goes beyond a chronological moment to a specially ordered or significant moment. For example:

Time to love	=	*divinely appointed* to love
Time to hate	=	*divinely appointed* to hate
Time for war	=	*divinely appointed* for war
Time for peace	=	*divinely appointed* for peace

Using this phrase helps us to see how God is in control. Even though events may happen that are not in line with His character, we know that He will work them out for good for those mentioned in Romans 8:28.

As I write this book, we are currently living in the state of a global pandemic, an economic downturn, and civil unrest due to the injustices of racial inequality and other injustices. We are experiencing turbulent feelings and emotions because of the uncertainty of our future. At the time these were questions: Will they find a cure or create a successful vaccine for the virus? Will there be true justice for the racist killers of those who were slain?

Will our economy bounce back? Will the elections run smoothly? Will we ever get back to some form of normalcy? [2]

Knowing that God is in control, and that this point in *time* we are living in is *divinely appointed* by Him, gives us much hope. God does nothing unintentionally. Everything He does has a purpose. We may not understand it, but "... *we know that God causes all things to work together for good to those who love God, to those who are called according to His purpose*" (Romans 8:28 NASB).

I was taught by (See Attached Appendix A) my first real pastor, AJ Shankle, on how to study the scriptures. He said to go line by line and precept upon precept. Understand that when applying the Word of God to your life, there is always a literal and a spiritual meaning. Please allow the Holy Spirit to help lead you and guide you into all Truth and understanding. (See Appendix A for a breakdown the verses in Ecclesiastes 3:2-8 (NASB, 2000).

ACCOUNTING FOR THE PAST

That which is has already been, And what is to be has already been, And God requires an account of what is past (Ecclesiastes 3:15 NASB).

The past is not as meaningless as people dismiss it as being. A lot of times we think that once something has happened, that this is it – it's over; it's behind us. There is nothing more we can do about it. However, God is not regulated by time

---

[2] * Note: vaccine December 2020, cops found guilty June 2021, economy returned slowly, insurrection on the capital Jan 2021, normalcy, new normal we are working on it.

because He is outside of time. He can require an account of what is past or hold us accountable for our past actions not repented for.

This is good news for us. He will hold an account of the things that were done to us in the past – slavery, injustice, unfairness, childhood trauma: God doesn't just let it go.

"To account for something" means to give it consideration or value. God gives our past consideration but wants us to leave that judgment to Him. He knows that we can and sometimes will dwell on the past. We sometimes define ourselves by our past. That is why He tells us in Isaiah 43: 18, *"forget those former things, nor consider the things of old"* (NKJV).

And Solomon is assured:

I said in my heart, "God shall judge the righteous and the wicked, For there is a time there for every purpose and for every work"
(Ecclesiastes 3:17 NKJV).

As I write, our country is going through civil unrest with protests due to police brutality and the killing of unarmed Black people. Reading and studying this scripture gives me hope, because it assures me that God will be the judge and will judge righteously. There is an appointed or divine time for every purpose and every work. There is a time for His judgment – His final say, His divine punishment. God has the final authority on any matter, especially judgment of the wicked and vindication of the righteous.

CHAPTER 2

NAVIGATING THE PLAINS

The Navigator

A navigator is a person who directs the route or course of a ship, aircraft, or other forms of transportation, especially by using instruments and maps.[3] In the Navy, the navigator is the person onboard a ship responsible for keeping it on course and on schedule. The navigator's primary responsibility is to be aware of the ship's position at all times. Their responsibilities include planning the journey, advising the captain of the estimated timing to destinations while en route, and ensuring hazards are avoided.[4]

Navigating through life would assume God the Father, Jesus the Son and Holy Spirit to be both Captain and Navigator. The Triune God is the One who charts the course toward your destiny and purpose. He knows how to plan your journey in life, how to estimate the timing to your destination, and ensure the hazards or stumbling blocks are avoided.

All the same, allowing God to be the captain and relinquishing the steering wheel of your life to Him can be challenging. Even though you know He cares for you and wants the best for you, trusting Him through those times when you can't see your way out is not easy. This is why Proverbs 3:5 says, *"Trust in the Lord with all thine heart, and lean not unto thine own understanding"* (KJV). Your own understanding will have you in despair and hopelessness because you don't see what He sees.

---

[3] Dictionary.Com, "navigator (n)" accessed June 15, 2020, https://www.dictionary.com/browse/navigator

[4] Mike Grieson. "Aviation History – Demise of the Flight Navigator, Franco Flyers.org website, October 14, 2008. Accessed June 14, 2020. https://www.francoflyers.org/2008/10/aviation-histor.html

Walking out this experience of being in shelter-in-place, having to wear masks, and adjusting to this new normal makes it difficult to understand how to navigate. But allowing God to be the Navigator is key to coming through with sanity and composure. Even without a pandemic, giving God the reins of our life is easier said than done, because we don't want to relinquish control. The Bible says that the Holy Spirit is our guide according to John's Gospel:

But the Advocate, the Holy Spirit, whom the Father will send in my name, will teach you all things and will remind you of everything I have said to you (John 14:26 NIV).

Jesus is talking to His disciples, and that includes us as His disciples here and now. As students, we must learn to see the lesson. What has this experience taught us? What did He tell us or show us while navigating a situation like this?

But when He, the Spirit of Truth, comes, He will guide you into all the Truth. He will not speak on His own; He will speak only what He hears, and He will tell you what is yet to come. He will glorify Me because it is from Me that He will receive what He will make known to you (John 16:13-14 NKJV).

Now there is fact and there is Truth. Fact is mostly based on evidence and science. But Truth surpasses evidence because it is based on faith in what the Word says. Truth is a Kingdom word. People will say things and state them as fact; however it is up to the hearer to believe in the evidence. The Holy Spirit is Truth and only speaks Truth. Because He is the creator, His

Truth is fact. For example, my bank account may say I am broke – fact; however God said He will supply my every need – Truth. His guiding us into all Truth implies guiding us into the reality of His Word – which will never pass away! God's Word is still creating in the universe. When He spoke "Let there be …" into the atmosphere, it released a continual process of creating. Navigating through this journey of life and all the in between moments is using the Word of God as a compass. This compass always points to True north.

The Holy Spirit is definitely the Navigator in my life, and the One who charts my course. We have to realize that God's understanding is nothing like our way of understanding. He will give us the revelation into something after we have gone through it. There are situations that have occurred in my life that I am still waiting to receive understanding about. However, I am stronger because of them. And I trust they happened for my good because He has said so in Romans 8:28.

THE PLAINS

In geography, a plain is a flat, sweeping land mass that generally does not vary in elevation. Plains occur as lowland along valleys or on the steps of mountains, as coastal plains, and as plateaus or uplands.[5]

In life, a plain is a continual movement forward without seeing a way or direction to exit or to move around. Walking in the plains can be monotonous as we circle around with no

---

[5] National Geographic, "*Plain*" accessed June 15, 2020, https://education.nationalgeographic.org/resource/plain

end in sight. For instance, you wake up in the morning, get dressed, go to work, come home, eat dinner and then go to bed; only to do the same thing the next day, all over again. You feel like you are in a continual cycle or treadmill; maybe you even feel stuck.

I have been in a place of wash, rinse, repeat for the past two years. I was told after eleven years of being on staff full-time at our church that my position would be eliminated. I was devastated and frustrated. A few months after that happened, we relocated our family from Northern California to Las Vegas. I had still not found a new job, a new church, or my "next" in life. My husband worked from home, and I would hear him on the phone, making deals, putting out fires and sometimes laughing with co-workers and friends. Then he would have to travel a couple of days a week, which would leave me home alone. In the meantime, I would be on LinkedIn, Indeed and other career sites, applying for jobs, tweaking my resume to fit the job descriptions, and updating my profile.

Then it got mundane. I would get the "We regret to inform you" emails or no response at all. I would search and pray every day for a position that would allow me to use my creative gifts and talents. I even bit the bullet and got a job at Macy's in the shoe department. I hated it. After two weeks, I quit.

I kept feeling like I was going backwards – that everything I had done prior to losing my job had all been for nothing. I think what got me at the Macy's job was when my manager pulled me aside for wearing denim. In my last corporate job, I was making a competitive yearly salary, and now I was at $9.00 an hour plus commission with a draw. My last check there was for $14.00, not even worth the gas money.

In my life up to then, I had never applied for over fifty jobs in a twelve-month period. And now it was fifty jobs and having absolutely nothing to show for it. Eventually, I stopped looking.

I am extremely grateful for my husband, our new home, and the ability to be in this space. But I felt my days adding up to the same routine. I then decided to change my focus from looking for something to creating something.

So, here I am writing this book about navigating through the frustrations, disappointments, triumphs, and opportunities while waiting for something new to appear. I chose the title, *The Journey In Between*, because it doesn't necessarily offer concrete solutions but more narrates my experience, and perhaps helps you to navigate your journey.

The essential point to navigating the plains is to stay moving forward. You assess where you are, by looking back every now and then, to see how far you have come and celebrating the baby steps. Eventually, you will notice you have walked up a hill. You look back and see your path or elevation and applaud the fact that you made it out of the plain.

Living in Las Vegas it gets pretty hot in the summertime. This day was in the 110s F, so my husband and I decided to drive up to Mt. Charleston to cool off. As we were driving, we flipped on the navigation in our car to the compass setting.

When we turned off the freeway onto the two-lane highway leading up the mountain, we noticed the outside temperature gauge dropping and the compass numbers rising in elevation above sea level. Because of our perspective on the road, we could not yet see our gradual climb. However, we did note the shift in our transmission as our car climbed up the mountain. As we looked back in our rearview, we were amazed at the incline. Then the terrain began to change, and we could now see the road ascending up the mountain.

While in the plains or even the wilderness, it is important to keep moving forward. The terrain doesn't change if you stay in the same place and keep going around in circles, like the over-used definition of insanity, doing the same thing over and over again and expecting different results.

As we were driving up the mountain, we could feel the strain on our car engine until my husband pushed the accelerator on that 300-horsepower, turbocharged 3.0-liter six-cylinder engine. Then it shifted gears and begin to make the climb. We have both the ability and the capacity to get through our plains and wilderness experiences if we trust the Holy Spirit to be our guide and our turbo booster.

The Holy Spirit will help us to climb out of the mundane of feeling stuck. He guides us to read the compass, like the scripture in Isaiah 43, which declares God is doing a new thing, and for us to not cling to past events or dwell on yesterday. And that new thing is springing forth, coming into play NOW! (Isaiah 43:18-19)

Keep looking upwards to the hills for that is where your help is coming from:

> *I will lift up my eyes to the hills—From whence comes my help?*
> *My help comes from the LORD,*
> *Who made heaven and earth.*
> *He will not allow your foot to be moved;*

Eileen Deadwiler

He who keeps you will not slumber.
Behold, He who keeps Israel
Shall neither slumber nor sleep
(Psalm 121:1-4).

I am comforted that He neither slumbers nor sleeps, so that I can have sound rest.

CHAPTER 3

TESTING IN THE WILDERNESS

ALL THAT IS IN THE WORLD

*For all that is in the world —**the lust of the flesh, the lust of the eyes, and the pride of life**—is not of the Father but is of the world* (1 John 2:16 NKJV, emphasis added).

Navigating through the plain can also be a wilderness experience. The wilderness is known to be a barren or a desolate wasteland. There is literally nothing there physically sustainable for you – no fruit trees, or water; no job, no community, and no friends.

However, in God's perspective it is space where He can be Lord. Because there are few distractions, you concentrate on your needs being supplied by Him. You can walk in the Spirit and not in the flesh. Spiritually, being in this state is a faith walk, trusting God that this is where He desires for you to be for now. He wants you to trust Him through it, and He will supply all that you need.

However, in your human flesh you resist this location because you want to have clout and influence, see results, or be in a position of authority and make money moves. You want to have thousands of social media followers and have your posts and videos go viral as affirmation that you made it.

In the wilderness, temptations and trials are also to be expected. The wilderness journey can cause you to withdraw into your feelings. The strange stillness of the setting can mess with your emotions and trigger you to spiral down and wallow in self-pity. Your flesh will be tempted to be satisfied by its demands instead of allowing God to be your provider.

When Jesus was led away into the wilderness by the Spirit to be tempted of the Devil, the Devil used the same three tactics he used to tempt Eve in the garden. They were: the lust of the flesh, the lust of the eyes, and the pride of life.

The enemy of our souls has not changed his tactics an inch, and he is still using this on us today. Why? Because it works! Especially if you are not led by the Spirit, your Navigator, you will not know that the antidote is this scripture, "*I say then: Walk in the Spirit, and you shall not fulfill the lust of the flesh*" (Galatians 5:16 NKJV).

LUST OF THE FLESH

Lust means to be consumed with an inordinate desire for something. You are constantly thinking about this thing. You can't shake it. You want this so bad, that you will do anything to get it. Lusts of the flesh according to Galatians are considered deeds of the flesh, which are contrary to the Spirit of God, for the flesh sets its desire against the Spirit and the Spirit against the flesh. (see Galatians 5:17).

> *So when the woman saw that the tree was* **good for food**, *that it was pleasant to the eyes, and a tree desirable to make one wise, she took of its fruit and ate. She also gave to her husband with her, and he ate* Genesis 3:6 (NKJV, emphasis added).

Eve saw that the tree was good for food. Our physical bodies (flesh) need nourishment or food to survive. The average human body can survive one to two months without solid food but no more than a few days without water. According to Matthew 4, Jesus was led away into the wilderness by the Holy

Spirit, where he fasted forty days and nights, to be tempted of the Devil.

Now when the tempter came to Him, he said, "If you are the Son of God, tell these stones to become bread" (Mathew 4:3 NIV).

I am sure Jesus was tempted to eat because He was hungry. The stones probably already looked like bread to Him because He was literally starving. His flesh desired and needed food.

Question: When is eating food a sin, Eve?

Answer: When doing so is disobedient or contrary to the will of God at that time.

One could argue that Jesus turning that stone into bread for His own selfish gain would have only benefited Him. Jesus did not come into this world to satisfy His earthly needs. He came that *we* might have life, not that "I, Jesus might have life." Jesus had to put His flesh under subjection to His spirit man.

But the main point is that the miracle move of turning stone to bread would have also glorified Satan because it was done at *Satan's* word and not the instructions of the Father. The Devil questioned God's Word just as he did with Eve in Genesis 3 … "Has God indeed said …?" or "If you are the Son of God …?" in Matthew 4. He always tries to get us to second guess, ponder or reason the Word of God using our own understanding compared to taking God at His Word.

The enemy tempted Jesus while His flesh was weak. His spirit was strong because He denied His flesh and was able to combat and resist the Devil. He resisted the temptation because He was waiting for the timing of His Father.

Notice that the Devil knew scripture and used it. Let us see how Jesus responded in every instance.

Jesus' Response 1

"If you are the Son of God, tell these stones to become bread," Jesus answered, "It is written, 'Man shall not live by bread alone, but by every word that proceeds from the mouth of God" (Matthew 4:3-4 NKJV).

The scripture Jesus referenced is from Deuteronomy 8:3.

He humbled you, causing you to hunger and then feeding you manna, which neither you nor your ancestors had known, to teach you that man does not live on bread alone but every word that comes from the mouth of the Lord (NKJV).

Jesus is saying survival is not always predicated on the sustenance of the flesh. Mankind is made up of three elements, soul, body, and spirit. No, it's only through fulfilling the needs of all three physically, mentally, and spiritually that we can enjoy wholeness. He humbled your flesh, taught your mind, and filled your spirit with His spoken Word.

Jesus endured this trial as man to show us that we have the power to withstand the temptations of the flesh if we stay connected to the Father and walk in the Spirit. Not living by bread alone basically implies that our flesh is humbled as we wait for God to provide for our needs. That teaches us to trust Him and have faith in the nourishment of His voice to give us life.

LUST OF THE EYES

*So when the woman saw that the tree was good for food, that it was **pleasant to the eyes**, and a tree desirable to make one wise, she took of its fruit and ate. She also gave to her husband with her, and he ate* (Genesis 3:6 NKJV, emphasis added).

Then Eve noticed that the tree was pleasant to the eye. Every flawless leaf was beautifully green, and each healthy branch was growing gorgeous mouthwatering fruit, good enough to eat. But though something looks good, it does not mean it is good for you.

Then the devil took him to the holy city and had him stand on the highest point of the temple. "If you are the Son of God," he said, "throw yourself down. For it is written: 'He will command his angels concerning you, and they will lift you up in their hands, so that you will not strike your foot against a stone'" (Matthew 4:5-6 NIV).

Just like he did with Eve, the Devil questioned Jesus' identity and wanted Him to prove His sonship.

Compare the above with what he said to Eve:

"For God knows that when you eat from it your eyes will be opened, and you will be like God, knowing good and evil" (Genesis 3:5 NIV).

The Devil in his craftiness lured Eve into thinking that God was holding out on her and Adam. That made her question their position in God as image bearers. If we are made in God's image then we reflect Him. There was nothing missing, nothing broken: they were perfect. The wilderness experience can cause us to question our identity in Christ too. "Am I not enough?" "Why is God holding out on me?" "Lord, if this is really You, give me a sign?"

With Jesus the enemy tried to get Him to prove His Sonship. This was the lust of the eyes, His identity. Your identity is how you see yourself. We prove who we are not just by showing our picture identification, but by accomplishing things to show our charter traits. How do you see yourself?

Jesus did not have to prove anything to the Devil, and neither do we. Just because you can do something, does not mean you should do it. This was also said by Jeff Goldblum in the movie Jurassic Park[6] about man producing dinosaurs.

The scripture the Devil quoted was from Psalm 91, such a personal Psalm to the one familiar with the secret place of the Most High.

For he will command his angels concerning you to guard you in all your ways; they will lift you up in their hands, so that you will not strike your foot against a stone (Psalm 91:11-12 NIV).

The Devil thought he had Jesus, by quoting scripture. "If You are who You say you are, the angels will catch you and protect you." Jesus is secure in who He is, which is why it is important for us not to compare ourselves with others. The Devil wants us to doubt our full identity in Christ. He wants us to be tempted to think we are missing something, and that we are not enough. With the lust of the eyes, what do you

---

[6] *Jurassic Park*, directed by Steven Spielberg (Amblin Entertainment, Universal Pictures, 1993)

see? What is your perception of yourself? Are you worthy enough for God to protect you? Do you see yourself as one the angels would rescue? Do you really find safety in God? The answer to all these questions is Yes!

This is always the temptation of seeing yourself other than how God sees you. We must come into agreement with God regarding how He sees us! We are made in His image. He formed man from the earth and breathed into man's nostrils the breath of life, and man became a living being. Don't throw yourself down to prove anything.

You have the breath of God flowing through you. Just inhale right now, go ahead take a deep breath in … then exhale, and let it out! That is the *ruach* breath of God! - *Selah*

JESUS' RESPONSE 2

Jesus answered him, "It is also written: Do not put the LORD your God to the test" (Matthew 4:7 NIV).

According to Gill's Exposition commentaries, tempting God, is requiring a sign of Him or miracles to be done by Him for personal gain.[7] Jesus is referring to a text in Deuteronomy.

Do not put the LORD your God to the test as you did at Massah (Deuteronomy 6:16 NIV).

At Massah in Exodus 17:7, the Israelites had quarreled and murmured against God provoking Him to give them

---

[7] John Gill, "*John Gill's Exposition of the Bible*," Christianity.com, 2022 accessed April 21, 2022, https://www.christianity.com/bible/commentary/john-gill/matthew/4

water while in the desert, by saying, "Is the Lord among us or not?" They knew He had delivered them out of the hands of the Egyptians. They tried it again in Numbers Chapter 11, wanting meat instead of Manna. So, God gave them quail, then struck all of them that complained with a plague before they could even digest the meat. He is the same God in the Old Testament as in the New Testament and even today. Jesus would not question that He was in the care of God and refused to throw Himself down into the arms of the angels at the Devil's command.

PRIDE OF LIFE

*So when the woman saw that the tree was good for food, that it was pleasant to the eyes, and a tree **desirable to make one wise**, she took of its fruit and ate. She also gave to her husband with her, and he ate* (Genesis 3:6 NKJV, emphasis added).

Pride is a selfish move, being boastful of your own achievements. God has nothing to do with this mentality: "I will be wise because I ate the fruit; I did this." Eve was deceived into thinking that eating the fruit from that tree would make her wise. She was already wise. As I stated earlier, she was made in the image of God which reflected Him. Nothing missing, nothing broken.

Again, the devil took him to a very high mountain and showed him all the kingdoms of the world and their splendor. "All this I will give you," he said, "if you will bow down and worship me" (Matthew 4:8-9 NIV).

The Devil knew the love Jesus had for mankind. By showing Him the realms of all the kingdoms below and their splendor, he could tempt Jesus with the heart strings. The fact that the Son of God would leave His throne in glory to dwell among man and would later sacrifice His life for us already proves that He loves us without a doubt.

Seeing the domain that Adam forfeited, this invitation to take back the earthly kingdoms could entice Jesus to bow to him. It could be persuasive to Jesus' flesh to regain the love of man and influence him to turn back to God without having to pay the ultimate sacrifice. The flesh does not want to die a humiliating death on a cross.

What does that look like for us? We see it every day on reality and lifestyle shows with product placement of high-end fashion and luxury toys. We see men and women cat fighting and being degraded and demeaned in their clamor for ratings while wearing Gucci and driving a Bentley. And if we want a little bit of that, without going through the proper patient processes of working, saving, and investing, we can find ourselves in debt by accepting all those quick credit card offers that come in the mail and our inboxes.

Trying to live a life that seemingly looks prosperous and famous, and having all the things you desire will make you happy for a moment. But at the end of the day doesn't the scripture ask, *"What will it profit a man if he gains the whole world and loses his own soul?"* (Mark 8:36 NKJV)

JESUS' RESPONSE 3

Jesus said to him, "Away from me, Satan! For it is written: 'Worship the LORD your God, and serve him only'" (Matthew 4:10 NIV).

Jesus demonstrated what we should do when the enemy comes at us in an overwhelming way. We must use our audible voice with the authority in Christ to command Satan to get away from me!

"Go! I am not worshiping you!" and immediately begin to praise God for His goodness and mercy.

There are certain lifestyles we would like: the big house with the two cars and a boat, but it means nothing if you are not content in your spirit and soul.

The pride of life isn't always about things. For Jesus, I believe the temptation was in His love for us, that could have enticed Him, but He knew the salvation plans of the Lord God were assured. And He knew it will take only His death and resurrection for man to be redeemed.

The pride of life is greed, desiring more than you need. It's prestige, wanting the influence of the so-called elite. It's privilege, having benefit and access in spaces just because you have the correct skin tone or affluence at the appropriate time. Again, just because you can, doesn't mean you should.

And because Jesus was tempted and overcame in this area, He will help us to overcome.

In that He Himself has suffered, being tempted, He is able to aid those who are tempted (Hebrews 2:18 NKJV).

For we do not have a High Priest who cannot sympathize with our weakness, but was in all points tempted as we are yet without sin (Hebrews 4:15 NKJV).

Jesus made it so that we don't have to fend for ourselves. His grace is sufficient. We can come boldly to the throne of grace because of Him.

Thank You, Jesus!
Thank You, Father, for Your grace.

Chapter 4
Into the Jungle

Even without all the calamities of 2020, life still happens. We had the tragic loss of the beloved athlete Kobe Bryant, along with his daughter and seven others, in a helicopter crash. My husband and I suffered the loss of his father. One of my closest and dearest friends succumbed to a heart attack. Our youngest daughter had back surgery to remove a tumor. Our middle daughter had to reschedule her wedding, our son enlisted in the Navy, and our oldest daughter adopted a precious puppy.

Life.

Yet through it all, God is still faithful.

It's Like a Jungle

Cue Grandmaster Flash:

"It's like a jungle, sometimes it makes me wonder how I keep from going under … hah hah hah hah hah."[8]

The jungle represents obstruction of view. Trees and bushes are like distractions and chaos. Navigating during this period felt like a wilderness of dense overgrowth, a jungle. The most interesting part was that the *whole world* was navigating the jungle pathways of this pandemic at the same time. Facing the chaos, loss, hurt, grief, anger – interspersed with the occasional joy and sunshine – with everyone at that same time was like a blessing and a curse.

We heard the blessing in the empathetic and compassionate commercials, like "We are all in this together," and "We got you." We applauded the essential workers: health care providers,

---

[8] Grandmaster Flash and the Furious Five, "*The Message*," October 1, 1982, Sugar Hills Records ®2004

first responders, truck drivers, mail carriers, teachers (online) and even grocery store clerks.

The curse, however, seemed to bring no relief. There was no one who had already been through it that we could lean on. Our pastors and spiritual leaders were leading while bleeding. Our churches were shut down due to lockdowns, so we had nowhere to congregate. The people we would normally lean on were just as inaccessible. Our government officials expressed their human frailty in the decisions that were made.

In all, we got a glimpse of a world seemingly without God. And yet He was there. He proved to be my stability in a world that was shaking and unpredictable.

In times of uncertainty, the enemy of our souls wants us to focus on our problems and fears. Ephesians 2:2 says he is the prince of the power of the air (and that includes the airwaves and media). The media kept showing stats of the virus and how many people tested positive and the death toll like a scoreboard by country. The media seemed to play up the drama as if by cue. We saw a man brutally murdered in 8 minutes and 46 seconds on screen, via phones, computers, and television. We saw people taking to the streets peacefully protesting, some looting, and unfortunately some rioting. We saw law enforcement shooting rubber bullets and tear gas at innocent peaceful protesters and militiamen (ordinary citizens with guns) storming the steps of a city hall because they felt their civil rights were violated. They wanted to open the economy and not have to wear masks.

Seeing all of this, I am sure caused most of us to have some kind of reaction. I felt it all – fear, anxiety, anger, rage, disappointment, sorrow, depression, and at times, hopelessness.

But then I began to wonder, "Lord what do You say about all this? You knew this was going to happen. Nothing is a surprise to You; there is no such thing as a crisis in the Kingdom of God."

Then my inner voice said, *'Be sober minded; be watchful. Your adversary the devil prowls around like a roaring lion, seeking someone to devour.'* (1Peter 5:8 KJV)

Even though all this is happening, and we are experiencing these occurrences, the enemy wants us to eat, live, and breathe it. He wants us to see it and think about it non-stop:

On the news – hear him roar!

On our Facebook, Instagram, and Twitter feeds – hear him gloat!

Discussing it with family, or friends or coworkers – hear him spread anxiety!

Speaking of it at the grocery store under our masks – hear him snigger!

But scripture tells us to be sober-minded and watchful because our enemy stalks us like a roaring lion looking for a likely victim. That can be challenging with perturbed voices and disturbing images constantly replaying on the TV. But we are children of light and heed the call to gird up the loins of our mind. We need to be sober-minded and watchful, as well as serious, sensible, and focused – not distracted or impaired, but clear-headed; not even skewed by our own biases.

As a Black American woman watching these images and hearing the tone of the messages broadcast, I'll admit I've been in my feelings. But again, I must turn to the Word of God to hear what is the Kingdom's response?

And be not conformed to this world: but be ye transformed by the renewing of your mind, that ye may prove what is that good, and acceptable, and perfect, will of God (Romans 12:2 KJV).

Not conforming to this world implies not allowing the world's reaction to the current events sway my view of the Kingdom of God's response. It also means renewing my mind. How do you renew your mind? With the Word of God.

Renewing our mind, is changing how we think. It means shifting our thought patterns about a situation, and having the ability to see God moving in all aspects of our lives and circumstances. God gives us a Kingdom way of seeing reality. At the same time, we don't have to negate our feelings. Those feelings are real – you can be scared, frustrated, or angry. Admit them, don't hide them under a mask. But also bring these emotions before the Lord and allow Him to work through with us.

And what's the Lord's prescription?

Rejoice in the Lord always: and again I say, Rejoice. Let your moderation be known unto all men. The Lord is at hand.

Be careful for nothing; but in every thing by prayer and supplication with thanksgiving let your requests be made known unto God.

And the peace of God, which passeth all understanding, shall keep your hearts and minds through Christ Jesus.

Finally, brethren, whatsoever things are true, whatsoever things are honest, whatsoever things are just, whatsoever things are pure, whatsoever things are lovely, whatsoever things are of good report; if there be any virtue, and if there be any praise, think on these things (Philippians 4:4-8 KJV).

I heard world-renowned minister and clinical psychologist Dr. Anita Phillips say, "'Be anxious for nothing' is not the eleventh commandment." In this scripture, the apostle Paul is giving us a strategy to work through our emotions. He is telling us not to approach life's uncertainties with worry and stress. God is your peace, and His presence is always there.

I personally have bouts with anxiety. I get these feelings of unease and nervousness about what could happen and even thoughts on the loss or death of loved ones or myself. During these episodes I become highly emotional and anxious about everything. For instance, after receiving a text from my kids or phone call from my husband, I imagine tragic events happening to them.

I am sure a lot of this is triggered from the traumatic occurrences from the pandemic of losing people and the unexpected loss of my dear friend. I could start reading into issues that aren't even there and it can be really hard to shake.

The world is in constant turmoil and there are many factors that have aggravated our anxiety levels: from country-to-country wars with Ukraine and Russia and threats of nuclear weapons being used in North Korea, to mass shootings hitting an all-time high with children dying at an elementary school in Texas, and innocent shoppers being shot at a grocery store in New York.

But in all this mayhem and chaos, whether personal or global, the Apostle Paul is telling us to rejoice in the Lord always. Rejoice in Greek is translated *chairo* (pronounced khah'-ee-ro), which literally means to be "favorably disposed to God's grace." [9] To rejoice in the Lord is to lean into God's grace always, in whatever circumstance or situation you find yourself in. How do you rejoice in the Lord when everything around is falling apart? Because our joy comes from Christ dwelling within us. Because in Christ we live, we move and have our being (Acts 17:28).

Then the Apostle Paul encourages us to be anxious or careful for nothing, that is, no thing. We don't have to worry about the "what if's" of a certain outcome because we can come to God **in everything** by prayer and supplication with thanksgiving and make our request known to Him.

It does not matter what it is, we can come to God. In everything! In our pain, in our grief, in our strife, our fear, our struggle, our distress, our anxiety. Why? Because we rejoice in the Lord, leaning on God's favor even while struggling or grieving.

How do we come to God? We use the vehicle of prayer and supplication with thanksgiving behind the wheel. We come to God driven with gratefulness and appreciation for who He is, what He has done, what He is doing, and what He is about to do. With an earnest, humble heartfelt desire, we invite Him into our affairs and release those affairs to Him by allowing Him to be Lord over them.

We then share our ask: what it is we are requesting. This could be healing of pain and disease, comfort for grief, restoration of our heart, protection for our families, provision

---

[9] Strong's Greek Bible Apps.com, "5463. Xaipw (chairo)", 2004 – 2018, accessed April 18, 2022, https://bibleapps.com/greek/5463.htm#str

for our material needs, or all the above at the same time. He is a big and great God!

SURVIVING THE JUNGLE

To survive the jungle, you must not only be defensive, but you should also fight offensively. There must be a strategy. The journey through the jungle is risky and can be wild. No creature is tame and may not fight fair. Navigating through this dense overgrown terrain will require new thought patterns, new strategies.

So a new mindset is needed.

> *You were taught, with regard to your former way of life, to put off your old self, which is being corrupted by its deceitful desires; to be made new in the attitude of your minds; and to put on the new self, created to be like God in true righteousness and holiness*
> (Ephesians 4:22 NIV).

You cannot maneuver this jungle with your old tactics and outdated map. That will get you walking in circles. Moreover, the jungle has many traps and man-eating predators and plants that desire to swallow you whole. Depression is such a predator. When one feels stuck and continues to spiral down in thoughts of despair it's like walking in quicksand. These are lies that are constantly being told by the enemy to keep your spirits sinking, far away from the God who saves through Jesus Christ.

The thick undergrowth of the jungle represents rotten lies and deceitful desires that are detrimental to health. It breeds plants of anger that give the Devil ammunition to lord it over you and keep you bound. Then there are overhanging creepers of bitterness, rage, and slander that produce the sour fruit of manipulation and malice in your relationships.

Can't see the forest for the trees...

Our enemy can assail us on all sides without notice. In fact, just as I was typing this, I got attacked. The enemy sat here and told me that I was stuck. "You have no life, you have nothing – a woman in your fifties without a job, without your own thing. Everybody has something to lean on and you have nothing. You don't have any income and your husband is frustrated with you. You don't even have a church or a community to belong to like you used to."

And I fell for it.

For a brief moment, I sat here and cried looking around in my oversized main bedroom with my neatly made California king-size bed and ten decorative pillows. I stared into my spacious bathroom with a vast sunk-in tub in between his and hers detached sinks and vanities, a separate walk-in shower and a closet large enough to fit a twin size bed. With all that I was wallowing about what I didn't have. Poor me! Sob!

God forgive me!

I could not see the forest for the trees. I could not see the big picture because I was looking at the details of what I "didn't" have instead of what I do have. I may not have the income yet, or the church home like I was used to, but I am in the process of writing a best seller (smile), a podcast that will attract a substantial audience and, most importantly, a husband and family that support my endeavors. I am focusing on where I am instead of the distant future. I did allow the fiery darts of the enemy to strangle my thoughts like wild chaotic jungle vines. However, I immediately began to cut them down with the Word of God, which is the sword of the Spirit, and declare Romans 8:37, "I am more than conqueror through Him that loves me."

Chapter 5
Guerilla Warfare in the Jungle

WARFARE IN THE JUNGLE

As we grapple with the jungle terrain, we can expect jungle warfare, or rather spiritual warfare. So to stay on our path in the natural, we must wear protective clothing and be alert to all the dangers. My prayer is that we are able to see the enemy for who he is, and defeat him by the Word of God, the blood of the Lamb and the word of *our* testimony.

Our journey through this terrain will require spiritual protection and a divine strategy to fight all that encounters and attacks us. The Apostle Paul gives us clear instructions.

Finally, my brethren, be strong in the Lord, and in the power of his might. Put on the whole armour of God, that ye may be able to stand against the wiles of the devil.
For we wrestle not against flesh and blood, but against principalities, against powers, against the rulers of the darkness of this world, against spiritual wickedness in high places (Ephesians 6:10-12 KJV).

To be strong in the Lord and the power of His might is to put our trust in His strength, not our own. We are to trust His military might, the power of His voice and His sovereignty over all things. For is He not the creator of all things, the One who made the heavens and the earth just by speaking them into existence?

So we are commanded to put on the whole armor of God, His whole protection, and whole covering that will deflect the attacks of the Devil. We can't just choose pieces of the armor as we see fit; no, we are to wear all of the six weapons. Each item works with the others to fortify us with His total support that will keep us from falling for the Devil's wiles just as the apostle Jude commits his life to "him who is able to keep you from falling" (Jude 24).

I call the wiles of the Devil, the "wilds of the Devil." "Wiles" are defined as "devious or cunning stratagems employed in manipulating or persuading someone to do what one wants."[10] Sounds very much like guerrilla warfare.

According to the New World Encyclopedia, "Guerrilla tactics are based on ambush, deception, sabotage, and espionage, undermining an authority through long, low-intensity confrontation."[11]

So the nature of guerrilla warfare is the slow, stealthy movements to sabotage us when we are least prepared rather than an open battle. In this sense, the enemy of our souls has used guerilla tactics to sidetrack us from who God has called us to be and to do, using intimidation and subterfuge against God's people.

To name a few of the enemy's sneaky tricks is ambushing our thoughts by feeding us with immoral and impure images. He raids our emotions by dictating lies about our feelings. He sabotages our relationships with strife and jealousy. He uses petty disputes and misunderstandings among our family members and churches. He assaults us with the hit-and-run memories of childhood trauma.

---

[10] Oxford Learner Dictionaries, "wiles (n)," accessed April 20, 2022, https://www.oxfordlearnersdictionaries.com/us/definition/english/wiles?q=wiles

[11] New World Encyclopedia, "Guerrilla warfare" accessed April 20, 2022, https://www.newworldencyclopedia.org/entry/Guerrilla_warfare

Satan's ploys will work if we are not geared up for his attacks. But God has given us a strategy not only to stand but to overcome and conquer. Even if we have been ensnared by the Devil, we can still come out unscathed in Jesus' name.

The Lord has warned us that this battle is spiritual, and we must fight using His tactics, through the Spirit and the Word. We must recognize that we are not dealing with human beings but we are up against high level demonic forces, which Paul describes as principalities, powers, rulers of darkness, spiritual wickedness in high places.

Who are these forces? They are a highly organized chain of command under Satan with different levels of authority and jurisdictions. Some govern nations, some regions, some global bodies, some individuals.

For we wrestle not against flesh and blood, but against principalities, against powers, against the rulers of the darkness of this world, against spiritual wickedness in high places (Ephesians 6:12 KJV).

PRINCIPALITIES

A principality (*archon* in the Greek) is the jurisdiction of a prince or principal ruler over a nation or an invisible realm. Satan is known as *"the prince of the power of the air, the spirit that now worketh in the children of disobedience,"* so he's the one in control over the mainstream media of a disobedient nation (Ephesians 2:2 KJV).

POWERS

Powers refer to those in authority who are empowered to rule and make moral decisions that affect people's lives. Think of those in authority in the senate, a school board or even a pulpit who are influenced by the enemy to institute changes contrary to our biblical values.

RULERS OF THE DARKNESS OF THIS WORLD

These are high level leaders at a global level who are empowered by Satan to make decisions and laws that affect a large section of humanity. They may control the banking system, healthcare system, the environment, or a global military oversight organization.

SPIRITUAL WICKEDNESS IN HIGH PLACES

Demonic spirits of evil in the heavenly realm that control major spheres of influence such as government, education, entertainment, communication, financial systems, causing them to uphold moral values that oppose God's righteous laws. One such sinister movement is towards global government enacting laws that restrict the freedoms of people, especially the right to worship and share the gospel.

In all this, we must understand that it is not people, or human institutions that are evil: it is the evil powers of darkness that control them and use them as their mouthpiece. That is why Paul warns us not to fight people, but to identify the demonic powers operating through them.

*For though we walk in the flesh, we do not war after the flesh: (For the weapons of our warfare are not carnal, but mighty through God to the pulling down of **strong holds;**) Casting down imaginations, and every high thing that exalteth itself against the knowledge of God, and bringing into* *captivity every thought to the obedience of Christ* (2 Corinthians 10:3-5, emphasis added KJV).

What is a stronghold? In the general sense it is a fortified place which becomes a place of refuge or protection. In this particular context, Paul is referring to a thought or belief system that is entrenched in our mind and controls our thought or desires. It could be a stronghold of addiction, or lust or violence that camps in a person's mind, or even a belief system that denies the Truth of the gospel. You see, if God is our stronghold, we uphold the Truth based on His Word. But if we deny the Truth of God's Word, we open ourselves to the infiltration of Satan's thoughts through what we read or see in society. As a result, we walk in deception.

The main thing we need to realize is that we are fighting an invisible foe, not people. When we find ourselves putting a human name or face to a situation we're going through, we're likely to miss the power of God. No, our battle is not with people: it's with the spirit of the enemy that's trying to penetrate our mind. Remember, Satan cannot really force his way into your mind unless you give him an entry point. Then he can come in and set up camp.

This leads us to discuss the importance of protecting our mind by putting on our Spiritual armor.

THE ARMOR

In this section we will discuss the whole armor of God that we were instructed and commanded to take up as our Spiritual weapons.

Wherefore take unto you the whole armour of God, that ye may be able to withstand in the evil day, and having done all, to stand. Stand therefore, having your loins girt about with Truth, and having on the breastplate of righteousness; And your feet shod with the preparation of the gospel of peace; Above all, taking the shield of faith, wherewith ye shall be able to quench all the fiery darts of the wicked. And take the helmet of salvation, and the sword of the Spirit, which is the word of God: Praying always with all prayer and supplication in the Spirit, and watching thereunto with all perseverance and supplication for all saints (Ephesians 6:13-18 KJV).

STAND THEREFORE

The first thing the Apostle Paul tells us to do after assembling the armor is **stand.** There is a stance or position a warrior takes in battle. Even boxers have a stance as they engage in the ring. It is all about your posture in your walk with Christ. You must be well balanced wearing all of the armor and not just the helmet and no breastplate.

For example, coming up against the enemy with just salvation and no righteousness, is like professing Jesus as Savior but not living a Spirit filled life. You will not stand. You have to wear it all. You want to make sure your footing is sure.

In this case you're standing on the firm foundation, the Rock, which is the Word of God. The Word is Jesus, and when we make Jesus our Lord, the gates of Hell will not be able to prevail. Jesus said:

> *"… on this rock I will build My church; and the gates of Hades (death) will not overpower it [by preventing the resurrection of the Christ]"*
> (Matthew 16:18 AMP).

Let's now look at the six pieces of armor. To explain our Spiritual armor, the apostle Paul used the analogy of the battle dress of the Roman soldier in his day.

LOINS GIRT ABOUT WITH TRUTH (BELT OF TRUTH)

The belt of Truth holds together all our mental faculties through the Word, so we will not be swayed by every wind of doctrine.

In addition, consider this. Our loins are considered "the region of the sexual organs, especially when regarded as the source of erotic or procreative power" (Oxford). There is power in procreation, because the Devil cannot create anything. He defiles, corrupts and adds confusion to everything that God in His glory deemed good and purposeful. Society now is in a moment of conflict over the issue of reproduction rights, protecting the unborn, defining gender and the sanctity of marriage.

Amid this vine entangled chaos, the Christian warrior is instructed to have your reproductive organs encircled with Truth, upholding God's design in His Word.

I heard a minister at a Christian conference for college students say it best, "Everything from your waist to your thigh, must tell the Truth about Jesus."

THE BREASTPLATE OF RIGHTEOUSNESS

The breastplate protects the vital organs within the warrior's chest, notably, his heart and lungs. The breastplate of righteousness doesn't fit on top of our achievements, for scripture says our own righteousness is like filthy rags.

All of us have become like one who is unclean, and all our righteous acts are like filthy rags ... (Isaiah 64:6 NIV)

No, our righteousness is not in our own filthy rags but in the righteousness of Christ. Just as Abraham's faith was credited to him as righteousness, our faith in the righteousness of Christ becomes our breastplate. This is the righteousness purchased for us by Jesus at the cross:

For He made Him who knew no sin to be sin for us, that we might become the righteousness of God in Him (2 Corinthians 5:21 NKJV).

The breastplate of righteousness will protect our hearts from pride that leads to making decisions based on our own strength and convictions. If we do so, the enemy will use our own weaknesses and vulnerabilities to penetrate our armor. But when we are covered with the breastplate of Christ's righteousness, the Devil does not see our weakness but sees the perfection of Christ . Therefore he must back off, even flee.

FEET SHOD WITH THE PREPARATION OF THE GOSPEL OF PEACE (SHOES OF PEACE)

The jungle floor can be tricky. There is quicksand, which looks deceptively like mud but when you step into it unknowingly, you find it is so water-logged, you can sink into it.

In this jungle analogy, if you are not walking with the intent of spreading the gospel of peace, you can find yourself sinking into an entrapment of chaos caused by the enemy. But when you have your feet covered with the gospel of peace, you are well prepared to counter chaos with the good news of the gospel. When we share the gospel with others through our conduct and personal testimony, we are walking in the serenity of knowing that we are bringing peace to every ground that we tread on.

Notice the great joy that came upon the people of Samaria when the evangelist Philip preached the gospel and performed great deliverance:

> *When the crowds heard Philip and saw the signs he performed, they all paid close attention to what he said. For with shrieks, impure spirits came out of many, and many who were paralyzed or lame were healed. So there was great joy in that city* (Acts 8:6-8 NIV).

TAKING THE SHIELD OF FAITH

The Roman shield was large enough to cover the body from head to toe. Wearing the shield of faith protects our entire being from the fiery darts of the wicked one. Not only do these darts pierce our body, they break out in flames on impact, causing, untold damage. For instance, the lies of slander and gossip can strike us and then spread like wildfire as we react. Other darts are hate, bitterness, and untamed anger that can lead to uncontrollable reactions – bursts of emotions that give rise to name calling, cussing people out, fighting, racist hate crimes, or even murder. As a society we see on the news frustrated and angry people at airports, on the freeways, give vent to rage and anger as their emotions get the better of them.

But we have a defensive weapon and that is the shield of faith in Christ's Word to resist all the attacks on our character and our safety. How do we resist these attacks? By placing our trust in the specific Word of God to counter the specific attack and then using our sword of the Spirit to speak against it. For example, when lies and slander are hurled at us we put up our shield using the right scripture:

"I am the righteousness of God in Christ" (2 Corinthians 5:21). "No weapon formed against me will succeed" (Isaiah 54:17). "What the enemy meant for evil, You, O Lord will turn around for good" (Genesis 50:20).

During the months after the public murder of George Floyd by a police officer, (who by the way has been convicted and sentenced to life imprisonment), I literally had to apply God's Word and keep my mind on Jesus. I was angry and frustrated that Black Americans, born and living in America still have to deal with this type of racist behavior from people who we are supposed to trust.

My deeper frustration came from the church leaders who I wanted to see united for this common cause of injustice, but instead saw a division because of different opinions. Fortunately, I had just started my virtual Bible study and we were able to discuss our annoyances and get Biblical insight on how to confront that evil, and this book is the fruit of that.

The more we hear the Word of God, the more our shield of faith is built up.

Consequently, faith comes from hearing the message, and the message is heard through the word about Christ (Romans 10:17 NIV).

Another great faith-builder is hearing testimonies of the great exploits and mighty acts of God from those who walked it out. When people tell of the goodness of God and how He delivered them from a life-threatening illness, saved them from certain death in a car accident or protected them from getting evicted, it causes our faith to soar.

AND TAKE THE HELMET OF SALVATION…

Salvation is the act of being saved from the consequences of sin which is death.

For God so loved the world that he gave his one and only Son, that whoever believes in him shall not perish but have eternal life. For God did not send his Son into the world to condemn the world, but to save the world through him (John 3:16-17 NIV).

The helmet of salvation is designated to protect the mind from doubt, deception and worry, among others. The enemy in the garden started with Eve by questioning God's integrity – "Hath God really said …" sowing just a pebble of doubt. In a court of law, if the judge or jury has reason to doubt the credibility of the key witness, the defendant gets a verdict of not guilty.

The helmet also guards our minds from unbelief. The pillars of Christianity are based on the solid belief in the Word of God which says. *"All Scripture is God-breathed and is useful for teaching, rebuking, correcting and training in righteousness* (2 Timothy 3:16). Remember how Jesus said to Peter, "*... thou art Peter, and upon **this rock** I will build my church; and the gates of hell shall not prevail against it*" (Matthew 16:18 KJV, emphasis added) It is upon this rock of the Word that the Church of Jesus Christ is built.

Your initial salvation is in believing and confessing Jesus Christ as the Son of God.

If you declare with your mouth, "Jesus is Lord," and believe in your heart that God raised him from the dead, you will be saved (Romans 10:9 NIV).

Your ongoing salvation is deliverance from harm by standing firm on God's Word in every circumstance. Hold on to the belief that you walk in righteousness and divine protection as you put on your helmet of faith every day.

... THE SWORD OF THE SPIRIT, WHICH IS THE WORD OF GOD

This is the best part about being a warrior is using the sword. I love the fact that the letters W-O-R-D are contained in S-W-O-R-D.

The jungle's wild creepers and dense undergrowth block our pathway, so that we must use the sword to hack down and clear a safe passage to travel through. We are able to wield the sword of the Spirit against the enemy as our only weapon of offense to pull down and split open the lies of the enemy.

For the word of God is alive and active. Sharper than any double-edged sword, it penetrates even to dividing soul and spirit, joints and marrow; it judges the thoughts and attitudes of the heart
(Hebrews 4:12 NIV).

Do you notice how Jesus fought back the enemy in the wilderness with the words, "It is written …" Every time the Devil came at Jesus twisting the Word, He countered the Devil with, "It is written …"

That is what we do with our offensive weapon as well. The Word of God – the Scripture, the Holy text, the Bible, the Logos (written word), and the Rhema Word (spoken Word) – is our sword of the Spirit. The sword is sharp and cuts going in and going out:

So when the enemy comes at us with the care of this life, you counter him by declaring aloud: "I will rejoice in the Lord, and not be anxious or worry because the joy of the Lord is my strength" (Philippians 4:4-6).

Then he tempts with the deceitfulness of wealth, and you tell him, "Silver and gold I may not have, but I have the power of the Holy Spirit. That power enables the blind to see, the lame to walk and the dead to rise" (Acts 3:6-7).

As he attacks with sickness and disease, we stand on "By the stripes of Jesus Christ, I am healed!" (Isaiah 53:5)

In order to fight with the sword, you must know the Word of God. Therefore, study the Word, meditate on it constantly, day and night and let it get into your innermost being.

But his delight is in the law of the LORD; and in his law doth he meditate day and night (Psalm 1:2 KJV).

Study to shew thyself approved unto God, a workman that needeth not to be ashamed, rightly dividing the word of Truth (2 Timothy 2:15 KJV).

PRAYING ALWAYS WITH ALL PRAYER AND SUPPLICATION IN THE SPIRIT, AND WATCHING THEREUNTO WITH ALL PERSEVERANCE AND SUPPLICATION FOR ALL SAINTS

The stance of the Christian warrior in the jungle against guerilla warfare is prayer in all humility – down on our knees. This fight is not about us alone; we are the army of God, so we must look out for one another. That is why I was so disheartened by the response (or non-response) of those church leaders regarding the social injustices and divisions during the COVID-19 Pandemic. The Bible clearly tells us in 2 Chronicles 14:7 what to do as the body of Christ:

If my people, which are called by my name, shall humble themselves, and pray, and seek my face, and turn from their wicked ways; then will I hear from heaven, and will forgive their sin, and will heal their land. Now mine eyes shall be open, and mine ears attent unto the prayer that is made in this place (2 Chronicles 7:14-15 KJV).

Our job is to humble ourselves to pray, seek the Lord, and ask for forgiveness for ourselves, our communities, our leaders. Then God will hear our prayers, forgive our sins (personal and corporate) and heal our land.

The enemy has really turned up the heat in this battle we are fighting. It is time that we understand as we journey through different terrain that we have ample protection with the full armor of God. When we the saints hold fast to the call of God upon our lives and use our weapons judiciously, even in the most difficult times, we know that in Christ we always WIN!

Chapter 6

Rivers in the Desert

THE DESERT

The desert for me represents a place of dryness. It is an extremely hot environment that, at times, can be very quiet and lonely. The quiet of the desert is like giving in to one's own thoughts: "Why am I here" and "What do I do next?" As we steer this journey in between and the terrain of the desert, I am reminded of the feeling I had after being told I was no longer needed on my job. Well ... what do I do now?

My desert experience was in trying to find out what to do next. Writing this book came from that exact experience. Feelings of loss, and uncertainty about my future, actually inspired something creative to be birthed. When my husband and I moved from California to Nevada it was from the Bay to the desert, literally, from surrounded by water to no water at all.

Seeing such a vast contrast, I began to question our decision, "God, why am I here?" I am reminded of what one of my favorite pastors used to say, with the biggest smile on his face, "God, what are You up to in this?"

God always seems to answer me in His Word. I've been blessed to open the Bible and find a scripture that speaks to me right away. Other times I've had to search the scriptures and then let the text marinate a while as a picture slowly begins to unfold.

That is what happened in this incident. I had begun my women's Bible study via Zoom, and the lesson was on the rivers in the desert. It was based on that familiar passage in Isaiah:

> *Do not call to mind the former things,*
> *Or ponder things of the past.*
> *Behold, I will do something new,*
> *Now it will spring forth;*
> *Will you not be aware of it?*
> *I will even make a roadway in the wilderness,*
> *Rivers in the desert ...* (Isaiah 43:18-19 NASB)

In the first line, God says to forget the former things; do not even think about them. Right away I knew to let go of my past. Yes, I was on staff at the church. Yes, I was productive in my ministry. Yes, I loved what I was doing. However, it was time to release it. All of it – the pain of being rejected, the hurt from having to leave my passion, and my disappointment in the leadership that I had so respected. The Lord said, "Do not even try to recall what you left behind."

Yet before the Lord even spoke to me in this quiet desert, all I did *was* think about it. I could not fathom why they did not want me. What did I do wrong? If anyone could fit into the new vision and new church administration, I thought it would have been me. And thinking like that made me sad and depressed. Then I went to the next part of the scripture.

God said, "Behold I will do something new!" "Behold" implies a great announcement or entry. God is announcing something is coming and He is about to reveal something new. He is moving and creating. The new represents a thing that has never been done before. Prepare for something different.

I held the scripture to my heart. He is doing something new in my life, something that I've never seen or done before. This is why He wanted me to forget the former things in the past.

The past represents what is behind you. When has looking in a rearview mirror allowed anyone to move forward? I mean, unless you're driving backward. By the way, don't drive backward.

The rearview mirror is there to help you see what is trailing you. It may be used to encourage you to speed up or get out of the way of a hurling distraction, but it's not to be gazed at continuously while moving forward. Your focus should be straight ahead. You can glimpse in the rearview only as a precaution.

However, if God is stating, "Do not call to mind the former things, or ponder about the things of the past," please know that obedience is in your best interest. Relishing in the "shoulda," "coulda," "woulda" does nothing but keep a person in a state of distracted daydreaming on what might have been. It can cause us to relive the disappointments and deferred blessings all over again. It's time to learn from the past, collect the tools from those experiences, and move on.

The scripture goes on to say **now** it will spring forth. "Now" means at this moment to quickly move from a restricted position to a forward motion. Something that was held back and hidden is *now* being thrust into plain sight.

What could that be? Something new, perhaps something that you weren't ready for because you were holding on to the past. Trust me, there are wonders on the other side of obedience.

God never asks a question He does not know the answer to. The following are three different Bible translations of the same question. He asks:

*"Will you not be **aware** of it?"* (NASB)
*"Do you not **perceive** it?"* (NIV)
*"Shall you not **know** it?"* (KJV)

Be aware, perceive and know. Are you not aware – in other words, are you not informed, cognizant, and mindful – of this new thing? Do you not perceive – see, recognize, and sense – it? Shall you not know – understand, comprehend, and be informed – of it?

God was telling me to pay attention and be mindful of what He is doing. This should be an intentional response to His presence. It is like walking into a room and immediately becoming aware of your surroundings.

We are to use all five senses in the spirit: sight, smell, taste, touch, and hear:

What do you see? Seeing here is faith in the Spirit. "Walk by faith and not by sight," (2 Corinthians 5:7 KJV).

What can you smell? Smell translates to sacrifice in the Spirit, a fragrant aroma. *"... just as Christ also loved you and gave himself up for us, an offering and sacrifice to God, a sweet fragrance"* (Ephesians 5:2 WEB).

What does it taste like? Something flavorful. Taste His goodness, *"Oh, taste and see that the LORD is good"* (Psalm 34:8 NKJV).

What does it feel like? Touched by God is healing from His virtue. Jesus said, *"Someone touched Me, because I perceived power going out from Me"* (Luke 8:46 NKJV).

What do you hear? There is a sound. Listening in the

Spirit. *"He who has an ear, let him hear **and heed** what the Spirit says to the churches"* (Revelation 2:17 AMP, emphasis added).

This journey has not been easy, as I am still in this stage of experiencing different things at various moments. But the silence of the desert helps with this process of the journey because it makes a demand on you to listen out for God.

As I was studying for this lesson, I also became aware of the diverse plants that survive in the desert. Maybe I could apply some of their survival characteristics steering through this phase of my life. As I did, I stumbled upon the term "drought escapers."

As we know the desert can be dry; even so the desert experiences drought. If it does not get the normal amount of rain it needs, as minimal as that can be, it can go into a drought. An article, *Surviving in the Desert* on the National Park Service website said this:

"Drought escapers cannot tolerate dehydration. Plant species escape drought by going dormant when favorable growing conditions disappear. These plants are usually annuals, growing only when enough water is available. Seeds produced under good conditions can lie dormant for years (years!) if conditions are not favorable for germination"[12] (emphasis added).

---

[12] U.S National Park Service, *"Surviving in the Desert"* Article April 19, 2018. Accessed June 23, 2020

Does that sound familiar? Sometimes God may have us going dormant because we may not be ready to bloom. The conditions aren't favorable ... yet. It's all about His timing, which, as we've already learned, is divinely appointed. His time is perfect for us. The desert season can be a time of protection, to be used as a period of preparation.

God then said, "I will make a roadway in the wilderness." A roadway is a map or direction or route that appears. He is saying He will guide us through that uncertain path, so we are not alone. There is a wonderful demonstration of God's concern for His people in the desert expressed in the book of Nehemiah:

You gave them your good Spirit to teach them to live wisely.
You were never miserly with your manna, gave them plenty of water to drink. You supported them forty years in that desert; they had everything they needed; Their clothes didn't wear out
and their feet never blistered (Nehemiah 9:19-2).
The Message Bible. (2002).

Rivers in the desert sound refreshing. Just picture it: trekking through desert sands, hot, sweaty, and panting with a dry mouth. Then you hear running water. You look up, baffled at what you see, thinking your eyes might be playing tricks on you. Behold, there before you is a beautiful thirst-quenching fountain of water gushing down the hillside.

---

https://www.nps.gov/articles/seug-desert-survival-strat.htm

A river is a natural flowing water source – in most cases fresh water – flowing towards an ocean, sea or lake.[13] Most rivers begin as small streams running from a mountaintop and fed by melting snow and ice, or rainwater flowing off the land.[14]

In the terrain analogy throughout this book, mountaintops represent those moments of blessing and victory that bring high praise unto God. Those experiences can fuel or feed into the streams that cause the flow of the river (or the oil of the anointing) that sustains and refreshes the weary traveler in the desert. This flow changes harsh conditions to cool and inviting. You are now hydrated and able to come out of your drought status.

This is the time to reflect on the goodness of God and how amazing He is. We're not dwelling on the former things any more. But we're remembering and acknowledging the attributes of God: His omnipotence (all powerful), His omniscience (all knowing), and His omnipresence (always everywhere).

> *Remember the former things, those of long ago;*
> *I am God, and there is no other;*
> *I am God, and there is none like me.*
> *I make known the end from the beginning,*
> *from ancient times, what is still to come.*
> *I say, 'My purpose will stand,*
> *and I will do all that I please'* (Isaiah 46:9-10 NIV).

---

[13] National Geographic Society "River" Accessed June 23, 2020 https://www.nationalgeographic.org/encyclopedia/river/
[14] Ibid

You will find that worship and praise unto our awesome God bring us strength and refreshing as we traverse this dry phase of our lives.

CHAPTER 7

AN ENCOUNTER IN THE VALLEY

WEEPING FOR A NIGHT

For His anger is but for a moment, His favor is for a lifetime; Weeping may endure for a night, but a shout of joy comes in the morning (Psalm 30:5 NASB).

After my career transition, we moved from renting a Bay Area house, to purchasing a gorgeous six-bedroom, five-bathroom home in North Las Vegas, Nevada. My husband travels a lot for work, two days here, a week there. His job also allows him to work from home, as long as there is an airport nearby, and Harry Reid (formerly McCarran) International Airport is twenty-five minutes out.

During one of his business trips, I was sitting on our oversized sectional at night in our new great room in the new house. The room still held the new paint and new carpet smell.

It was early 2019. Our youngest daughter was away at college. We had not yet adopted our dog, Dexter. I loved my house and was extremely grateful for what God had blessed us with.

But I felt an overwhelming loneliness.

In our move, we had left behind our children. Yes, grown adults, but still my babies. We had also left behind what we call our chosen family, great friends, who were closer than true family. And our church family, our community and support.

I had no job, no church, and no family with me, outside of my husband. I knew no one and I had no community I could lean on.

I would normally call my mother. However, in the fall of 2017, my oldest brother had passed suddenly. My mother was still grieving this terrible loss, and I truly felt I couldn't burden her. And yet I couldn't shake this sadness.

I broke. I began to weep.

It was a deep cry. It caused me to slide right off the couch onto our new soft padded carpet. I began to cry out with a great big howl.

"WHY!?

"Why did you take my brother, which caused so much sadness in our family?

"Why am I here alone?

"Why am I in this in between space suddenly at my age?" I had just turned fifty in November. I could not understand why I was starting over.

"Why, God?

"Why did you take *my* job? I worshiped You. I ministered for You. I served Your people. Why?

"I loved what I did. I enjoyed leading the congregation in worship, directing the choir, seeing lives changed through the ministry. And I was good at it.

"Why did I have to leave my children? I adore my children and being around them is exciting. I love watching them become who they are as young adults.

"I left my friends, my close friends that became family. Awesome women I invested time in getting to know, women who also poured life into me. So again ... why?"

I probably prayed and cried for a good two hours.

I had officially arrived in the valley.

THE VALLEY

According to the Encyclopedia Britannica, a valley is a low area between hills or mountains typically with rivers running through it. Valleys may occur in a relatively flat plain or between ranges of hills or mountains.[15]

In the spiritual context, a valley is the terrain in between the experiences of high points. Examples of high points are finally going back to school to finish your degree and receiving a well deserved promotion with a substantial raise. And the middle is the valley of trying to get to the next high point.

The valley is navigating change that happens suddenly, and you have little to no control over it. It can be traumatic, especially if you don't see it coming. Maybe you are productive on your job. Your performance positively affects the bottom line. You feel safe and secure.

I remember this feeling. I had felt it all at my last job – my lost job.

In the valley, you feel hopeless, stuck and, at times, disoriented because the terrain is depressed, surrounded, sunken in, unfamiliar. For me the walls of loneliness, personal disappointment, grief, and rejection felt like they were caving in on me.

I became depressed and began to spiral down into feelings of hopelessness.

---

[15] Baker, V. R.. "valley." *Encyclopedia Britannica*, March 21, 2020. https://www.britannica.com/science/valley. Assessed June 30, 2020

Pausing Isn't Pretty

So how do you gain momentum in the valley? How do you propel yourself out of the hopelessness, the grief, the depression?

The true answer is ... you don't.

Instead, you have to learn to embrace the pause. Sure, you can find quick fixes and band-aids that will cover the discomforting void, things that will temporarily move you forward. But, inevitably, you'll always end up back in the valley, the land of no momentum, of no forward progress, a place of despondency.

A pause.

In the movies of medieval battle scenes soldiers fought in hand-to-hand combat with swords or bayonets. They would fight all day, and at night there was a truce or break to collect their dead and wounded. They would rest, regroup, rebuild their strategy and start back fighting the next day.

The valley isn't glorious. It allows you to see the carnage of your past battles. Look at Ezekiel's vision of the dry bones in the midst of the valley (Ezekiel 37). In this text, the Spirit asked Ezekiel, "Can these bones live? Is there life left; is there hope in this place?"

For most of us, the year 2020 brought incredible amounts of loss and grief. For my family, it began with the loss of our patriarch, my husband's father, Birdie, who was the pillar of the Deadwiler family. A month later one of my dearest and closest friends, LaTanya Broadnax, succumbed to a heart attack.

A couple of weeks after that we then found out that our youngest daughter had a tumor under her spine that needed major surgery. In the midst of everything, we were dealing with a global pandemic, civil unrest nationwide, and a toxic political climate. It felt like the whole world was walking through the valley of the shadow of death at the same time.

But the valley is a deliberate place. It is the space to heal your brokenness, rest in God through worship, regroup in the revelation of who God is to you at this time, and rebuild your faith to trust the process.

Take comfort. It's only a pause in life, not the end. It's a temporary halt. It is a time to meditate, catch your breath and get your bearings. We are only to walk through the valley of the shadow of death, not stay there.

EMBRACE THE PAUSE

Every valley shall be raised up, every mountain and hill made low;
the rough ground shall become level, the rugged places a plain.
And the glory of the LORD will be revealed, and all
people will see it together.
For the mouth of the LORD has spoken (Isaiah 40:4-5 NIV).

If God says the valley will be raised up and exalted, He is saying you won't be in the valley too long. Is it here where we "embrace the pause"? Does it mean we genuinely accept the place we are at in this moment? It leads me to think I will get out of it quickly – there's an eject button.

But we all know sometimes the valley seems loooooooong.

But uncomfortable as it is, the valley is just as much an ordained place as the mountain and hill. "Every valley will be raised up, every mountain and hill made low," could signify a balancing, to be evened out so that all levels are equal as God designed their purpose to be, one not better or worse than the other.

No matter what length of time, long or short you're at in any particular level, mountain high or valley low, it is an intentional space God created to deepen your growth.

The Spirit told Ezekiel to speak to the dry bones. Why? Because God gave us authority over our situation to speak to the problem, to declare His marvelous works. I heard the preacher Creflo Dollar say, "Don't talk to God about your problems, talk to your problems about God."

A light bulb went on. Embracing the pause meant to embrace God's presence in my loneliness. Embrace God's approval of me. Embrace the comfort of the Holy Spirit. Embrace His acceptance of me.

Just like Ezekiel, we must prophesy over the elements in our valleys, no matter what is there. That is how God exalts the valley. Speaking God's Words into the atmosphere is activating life. Is there grief in your valley? Speak to it. Is there depression in your valley? Speak to it. Are there dead dreams decaying in your valley? Speak resurrecting life back into them.

During creation everything was formed with the spoken words in Genesis, "And God said let there be …" and then in Proverbs 18:21 says, "Death and life are in the power of the tongue." He gave us dominion and authority on the earth to speak to our mountains, impossible situations, and whatever is binding us in the valley. He gave us authority to prophesy life to the circumstance, and death to depression and misery.

I remember being in the hospital waiting area while my twenty-one-year-old baby girl was having surgery. It was in the middle of the pandemic, so my husband and I could not be there together. He had to wait outside in the parking lot. All I could do was worship.

I was still numbed by the deaths of my father-in-law, my friend, and the thoughts of my brother. My flesh could not take any more, and yet my spirit was on fire.

But I remember an overwhelming peace as I read the text messages of prayers and Facebook posts for my little one. I will never forget the phone call from my sister girl Coco, who had walked through similar situations with her daughter. She called me and prayed with me over the phone.

In some instances, in the Bible, a memorial was built to identify a location where a miraculous event or battle had occurred. In my valley, there was definite evidence of a battle. There were scars and fallen bodies all around me. But God let me know then, in that hospital waiting room, on that phone call, that this was just a walk.

Yes, we were going to make a memorial here and it was to celebrate the dry bones living again.

Chapter 8

Lily of the Valley

The Gospel According to Dexter

I wasn't a dog person – well, actually I'm still not. I can't even go to a dog park without anxiety. So I'll admit when my husband Derrick brought Dexter home on Father's Day of 2019, I was furious. All I could think about was my new carpet, my new furniture … in my mind, we had just lost our freedom as empty nesters.

He was a handsome hot mess in the beginning. He snatched my decorative pillows off my couch. He played keep-away, with us running around the house after him. And he was so athletic, he cleared our four-foot-high sectional. Backward.

In no time, this precious caramel-colored, brown-eyed, Boxer-Pit mix puppy won my heart over. He is such a lovable protector and companion for us. I believe it was God's plan for us to have him. Especially after the losses we experienced.

Dexter was a Godsend. He sensed our sadness, our frustrations, our fears. His attentiveness and affection showed when he gently lay his head on our laps or gave a paw of concern and soft licks and cuddles at the right time.

As I am writing this, I am preparing to launch my podcast also entitled *The Journey in Between* with Eileen Deadwiler. One of the upcoming segments is called *The Gospel According to Dexter: Life Lessons Learned Through the Experience of Having a Dog.*

My family's, and my own, experience in the valley was one of loss, of grief, of uncertainty, and of fear. However, Dexter's arrival was an unexpected, beautiful ray of light and comfort. He became living proof that God can use anything to work all things for our good.

But let's be clear. I'm not a dog person.

LILY OF THE VALLEY

On December 8, 1867, Charles Spurgeon described Christ in this manner so eloquently in his sermon, *The Rose and the Lily*:

"Christ is the beauty in the midst of a trial, depression, a low point.
He is the focus!

He stands out, He is Holy, worthy to be praised, honored, worshiped.

He is precious, He is the corner stone, He is the rock of our salvation

We regard Him as a luxurious delicacy, as rare and ravishing delight, comparable to the rose and the lily.

Yes, He is lily to you and me, poor dwellers in the lowlands. Up yonder he is a lily on the hill-tops, where celestial eyes admire him; down here in these valleys of fears and cares, he is lily still as fair as in heaven." [16]

In the Bible the lily of the valley is constantly used as a metaphor for Christ. In Song of Solomon 2:1, the woman declares, "I am a rose of Sharon, a lily of the valleys." Her

---

[16] Spurgeon, Charles, H. "The Spurgeon Center for Biblical Preaching at Midwestern Seminary." *The Spurgeon Library*. 2017.
https://www.spurgeon.org/resource-library/sermons/the-rose-and-the-lily/#flipbook/ (accessed June 30, 2020).

lover replies, "Like a lily among thorns is my darling among the young women." In the midst of pain and disorder, this lovely innocent white flower stands out in his eyes, and outshines that of all other women. Christ is the Lily of the Valley. He the light in the darkness, a delicate white flower blooming in chaos. When we place our focus on Christ rather than the circumstances surrounding us, He is able to grow and flourish inside of us, even in the hardest of times.

How do we focus on Christ in the valley?

We focus on Him being the center of our attention, despite the environment.

We focus on believing He will show up with the gift of living water to sustain us, even when we are dry and thirsty.

We focus on Him calling us out of our stuff. Like pain. And calling us to have a conversation.

We focus on seeing Him larger than our struggles.

When Jesus shows up in Samaria, He brings that kind of encounter to an unsuspecting, desperate woman.

AN ENCOUNTER WITH THE LILY (JESUS)

So, he came to a town in Samaria called Sychar, near the plot of ground Jacob had given to his son Joseph. Jacob's well was there, and Jesus, tired as he was from the journey, sat down by the well.
It was about noon.
When a Samaritan woman came to draw water, Jesus said to her, "Will you give me a drink?"
(His disciples had gone into the town to buy food.)
The Samaritan woman said to him, "You are a Jew and I am a Samaritan woman. How can you ask me for a drink?"

(For Jews do not associate with Samaritans.)
Jesus answered her, "If you knew the gift of God and who it is that asks you for a drink, you would have asked him and he would have given you living water" (John 4:6-10 NIV).

Jesus was tired from traveling. His weariness was not only physical, but it was also more like Him saying, "I must pass this way to fulfill my mission and I don't have a lot of time." He may have been exhausted from the synagogue with its cultural divisions and strife.

Samaria was a place of such division too. The Samaritans were a mixed race of people stemming from the intermarriages of foreigners and the remaining Jews left in Assyria. The result was a mixed religion, partly Jewish and partly idolatry. The so-called pure Jews despised them because they felt those intermarried Jews had betrayed their people and nation, and proper Jews would avoid travel through Samaria.

As outcasts, the Samaritans had set up an alternative center of worship on Mount Gerizim corresponding with the temple at Jerusalem.

However, Jesus refused to be restricted by cultural limitations and unspoken boundaries.[17] Limitations of racism, sexism, church divisions and denomination rivalries did not deter Him. His route through Samaria was His purpose.

He said to her, "Go, call your husband and come back." The woman answered and said, "I have no husband" (John 4:16-17 NIV).

---

[17] Zondervan New American Standard Bible. *Zondervan Life Application Study Bible: New American Standard.* Grand Rapids, MI: The Zondervan Corporation, 2000.

Jesus purposely made this detour to minister to a woman who was stuck in the perplexity of life. She had five husbands. Five! That's five different marriage lives! A merry-go-round of trying to find a sense of belonging!

And the man she was currently with was not her husband. Were they engaged, or was it a situation? When Jesus told the woman to go call her husband and come back, He knew about the previous five husbands and the relationship she was currently in.

He was saying in effect, "Call off your counterfeit covering and let *Me* deal with the state you are in right now. Allow Me to show you true intimacy, exposing the darkness in the valley with the light of Truth."

Jesus aiding us in the valley uncovers the deep hurts and secret sins that we've attempted to hide and cover with our own fig leaves. Because Jesus as the Lily of the Valley is the bridegroom of the Church, He wants to restore His bride to a place of worship in Him.

He is the covering from the storm, and protector from the lies that are contrary to what He says about us.

TRUE WORSHIP

"But an hour is coming, and now is, when the true worshipers will worship the Father in spirit and Truth; for such people the Father is seeking such to worship Him" (John 4:23 NKJV).

We are encouraged and strengthened through the valley with acts of worship, as we focus on Christ, the Lily. He is the beauty amid turmoil and confusion. He is standing, with outstretched arms like blooming petals, extending an invitation to be embraced. He is fixated on His love for the ones He redeemed through the ultimate sacrifice of His life.

We acknowledge His greatness, which is greater than the majestic mountains, by focusing on Him, not our feelings or circumstances.

World-renowned worship leader Joseph Garlington said, "True spiritual worship will cause God Almighty to come and sit with you, for He is enthroned in the midst of your praises."[18]

Worship is Spirit driven. We must put our flesh into subjection because it wants us to concentrate on feelings and wallow in a state of prolonged grief and sadness that can lead to depression. Countering the feelings of hopelessness with the Word of God is a weapon against our own flesh. And we can use it in the valley:

I am sad. ➜ He is my Joy.
The joy of the Lord is my strength (Nehemiah 8:10).

I am hurting. ➜ He is my comfort.
Your rod and your staff, they comfort me (Psalm 23:4).

I am weeping. ➜ He dried my tears.
God will wipe every tear from our eyes (Revelation 7:17).

I am grieving. ➜ He will uphold me.
God will uphold me with His righteous right hand (Isaiah 41:10).

---

[18] Garlington, Joseph L. *Worship, The Pattern of Things in Heaven.* Shippensburg, PA: Destiny Image Publishers, Inc., 1997.

I am frustrated. ➜ He is my peace.
May the God of hope fill us with all joy and peace (Romans 15:13).

I am weak. ➜ He is my strength.
God is our refuge and strength (Psalm 46:1).

These are not just words of affirmation: they are words of Truth. The Lord is joy. The Lord is peace. And He is a comfort to those who need Him.

As Darlene Zschech said, "Worship is the most selfless experience that your nature is capable of because it takes your eyes off of your weakness and on to God's power."[19]

That is what we are to do while traversing through the valley: look out for the Lily of the Valley, Jesus. Through worship I was able to steer my thoughts from my shortcomings and what I lost – even my grief. I began to see my journey more clearly and God's plan to give me hope and a future (Jeremiah 29:11).

---

[19] Zschech, Darlene. *Extravagant Worship*. Bloomington, MN: Bethany House Publishers, 2001. 99

CHAPTER 9
MOUNTAIN TO MOUNTAIN TOP

For Purple Mountains Majesty

Mountains are majestic and awesome. The peak of the mountain allows for breathtaking views of the valleys below as well as the surrounding mountain ranges.

But mountains can also be intimidating. While it is wonderful to gaze at a mountain in the distance, no one climbs a mountain accidentally. Mountains are scaled purposefully. To navigate the mountain terrain is a test of physical, mental, and spiritual stamina. But the climber has only one purpose: to make it to the top, to finish what they set out to do.

One cannot take the climb lightly because it requires preparation. Chase Tucker, an avid mountain climber and expedition leader, founded and created a training program that instructs on exact exercises to build a body that is ready for the mountains and to have the mental strength and motivation needed to be successful.[20] In his article, *Mountaineer Mindset*, Tucker discussed several mental qualities of winning climbers and how these qualities are evident in successful people as well.[21] He states, "The majority of the climbers on Everest are successful CEOs, entrepreneurs and wealthy individuals because the qualities developed in these lifestyles lend themselves to the mountaineer mindset, and

---

[20] Tucker, Chase. *Base Camp Training*. "*Mountaineer Mindset.*" basecamptraining.com. July 12, 2018. https://basecamptraining.com.au/2018/07/12/mountaineer-mindset (accessed August 31, 2021).
[21] Ibid

not only because they can afford it, (it costs over $60,000 to climb Everest)."[22]

THE CLIMB

Three of the four gospels – Mathew, Mark and Luke – describe how Jesus, after sharing with His disciples about His death and resurrection, led three of His inner circle up on a high mountain to pray.

Throughout His life on earth, Jesus would escape from the crowds to be alone to pray and commune with His Father. As believers, we should all adopt this "retreat" habit to help develop our own personal relationship with the Father.

I wonder what that hike was like for those three disciples, ascending above the busyness of the world with Jesus leading the way. Were Peter, James, and John wondering, where Jesus was taking them? Or were they familiar enough with His ways, and didn't even question Him? No doubt they found it a privilege to go on such a trip with Jesus!

They had no hiking boots or ropes. They might have been traveling on a path not used by others. Then they trekked to a height where they were able to break away from the marketplace and villages, to escape from the distraction of personal affairs and professional obligations. We should all take those intentional moments to spend time with Jesus.

---

[22] Ibid

TAKE A HIKE

This reminds me of a hike I went on several years ago. It's a bit embarrassing, retelling this story. My attitude was, well, less than stellar. But it paints a picture. So here we go.

My life group leader from church organized this hike with just us ladies. She scheduled our adventure a few weeks in advance so we could prepare. The hike was a popular spot called Mission Peak, a popular six-mile trail in Fremont, California. The trek to the summit is approximately two hours of well-traveled paths and attractive landscapes.

What I like most about the trail are the level plateaus that allow your legs to rest from the steady incline. We met at six in the morning at the baseline of the trail to gather and pray. I was excited as I had heard the stories of this trail and its views. We began the hike.

As we were walking, we commented on the gorgeous sunrise as joggers slipped by us, trotting up the trail. I was impressed. As we continued our climb, most conversations stopped because we had to concentrate on our breathing, while our quads and calf muscles burned like fire.

Here comes the embarrassing part. I began to complain, and I was the worst. I was like, "When is the next plateau? How much further do we have to go? Whose idea was this?" I was just awful! Every time I spoke up during the hike, it was a complaint or negative comment. I wonder if any of the disciples traveling with Jesus felt the way I did. I have a feeling Peter might have been the one to ask Jesus how much further they had to go, considering he was a fisherman and not a mountaineer. Just a thought.

As a leader, I was not a good example at all. When we reached the plateau, I asked if we could stay here and call it a day. It was high enough to see the landscape below, "So let's just wrap it up" I suggested. Our leader said, "No, we can make it. Let's go, ladies."

At the next plateau, which was actually the halfway point, we saw those joggers who had passed us, now on their way down. I felt defeated. I wanted to end the hike and go back down too. But yet again, our leader ignored me, and encouraged us to keep moving. I am sure Jesus probably said the same to His weary travel companions.

Finally, we reached the base of the summit. The grooved trail had ended. Now, we had to – yes, literally – climb up the slope using etched-out rock as stepping stones. The ladies who had climbed this part before led the way, and the rest of us followed their footing and hand placement. We finally got to the top, as those who were before us reached down to help pull us up. (That's a message right there, huh? Buy my next book. It's a doozy.)

At long, exhausted last, we made it! And y'all, it was amazing! You could see the whole valley: the entire San Francisco Bay, from San Jose to San Francisco. Simply gorgeous! Then it dawned on me, I could see why Jesus would escape to such a place: it was so peaceful, so above it all.

At the summit, stood a large cross, which we gathered around to pray and reflect on our journey. I was so grateful to be there and thanked God I had made it to the top. A few of the ladies called me out on my complaining. We laughed about it then, but they have never let me live it down.

And for the record, the way down was much faster. It took about forty-five minutes!

Discipline

Negotiating the terrain of a mountain requires discipline. Discipline, in turn, requires training and preparation. Habits of following a strict routine, mental fortitude, and self-control have to be cultivated and maintained way before the actual climb begins.

In this journey in between, there will be spiritual mountains we have to climb. Some may be small; others may seem monumental and unscalable. We can circle around them over and over, looking for shortcuts and loopholes, tunnels to cut through to the other side. We can pour out a bunch of energy looking for ways to NOT climb. But if we get honest with ourselves, the only way for us to grow is in the climb.

Sometimes … and let's face it, most times…

We're all going to have to climb.

And the only way to do that is to spend regular time in prayer alone with God.

In the same sense, spending time in prayer alone with God also requires discipline. We hear the phrases in church of "going higher in God." Going higher in God means to take a posture of Spiritual discipline by focusing on who God is, seeking understanding of how the Kingdom of God operates through Scripture, and listening to the voice of the Lord through the Holy Spirit.

Jesus often went away to pray. Training oneself highlights the importance of instruction and drill towards a specific end, in this case, going to another level in your walk with the Lord.

Essentially going higher in God is all about faith. Faith incorporates both nouns and verbs, implying concrete action towards a desired goal. Hebrews 11:1 says, "Now faith is the *substance* (noun) of the things *hoped for* (verb), the *evidence* (noun, "the process") of the things *not seen* (verb)." Faith is a discipline in and of itself.

In another article on climbing mountains, I couldn't help comparing the preparation required to climb a mountain to the preparation we must experience in our own spiritual walk. It struck me just how parallel the two really are.

In the article *How to Climb a Mountain*, Matt Barr another passionate mountaineer, recounts an interview with British climbers Mr. Neil McNab and Mr. Andy Perkins. In it, they detail the most successful way to prepare for a climb, using the following five techniques:[23]

Plan your campaign
Acclimatize (adjust to the climate)
Travel light
Watch out for weather
Get down alive

Let's dive into each of these techniques to see how similar they are to our own spiritual "climb."

PLAN YOUR CAMPAIGN – PLAN YOUR CONSECRATION

---

[23] Barr, Matt. *The Journal Lifestyle*. *"How to Climb A Mountain."* MrPorter.com. September 14, 2016. https://www.mrporter.com/en-fr/journal/lifestyle/how-to-climb-a-mountain-678460 (accessed August 31, 2021).

For climbers, planning means to do your research on the mountain you plan to climb, and investigate the touring companies and packages that best suit you.[24] Most importantly, prepare your mind, body and soul, remembering that climbing is mental and spiritual as well as physical.

In your dedicated time alone with God, planning is just as essential. Plan your mission or crusade with a prepared space and set time you would like to commit to earnestly seeking the Lord. Let your family know, especially any loved ones in your own house, that you will be spending time before the Lord for, let's say, two weeks at a particular place. If you are unable to leave, create a prayer closet in your house or a space designated for this time.

Jesus went away to pray. He was intentional in separating Himself from the world to connect fully with God. Just like aiming to lose weight or toning our body, we should set a goal for spiritual change. Having a start time and duration for this kind of campaign with the Lord is important and will enable you to develop habits with greater success.

Then map out your structure. Will you be fasting during this time of consecration? If so, how long and what will you be fasting: food, entertainment, social media, sweets, coffee, etc.? I grew up old-school, so we fasted food and all forms of entertainment, from sunup to sundown. Schedule your study time and have a journal ready to write down what you hear from God and scriptures that resonate. Again, this is a time daily or weekly to pray and commune with God without any distractions. Turn off your cell phone and maybe even your Wi-

---

[24] Ibid

Fi. Make this strictly uninterrupted time, set apart with the Lord. Map out time for praise and moments of worship, acknowledging God for what He has done and honoring Him for who He is. Maybe have others intercede for you during this period.

I am reminded of a woman, Mother Elizabeth Juanita Dabney, a National Mother and intercessor for the Church of God in Christ. She made a covenant with the Lord to meet with Him every day in prayer for three years at the same time and place. The enemy tried to stop her through sickness, loneliness, witchcraft, and ridicule from others; yet she continued. She wasn't even aware that her three years were over, and as she went to the place to pray, she heard the Lord say, "Go home, your three years are up; you have prayed through into My Glory."[25]

When she finally went home, God met her there. She recounts a manifestation of His Glory so heavy all she could do was surrender.

"A spigot turned on in the ceiling and the oil of the Lord ran upon me until I was encased about eight inches thick. It was like being placed in a closet. I was to that place I could not think, all human help had disappeared, my flesh and self-nerve offered resistance – this was a glorious scene. Satan knew the Lord was preparing me for this prayer battle. He told me I would strangle to death. I had always especially feared death by strangulation or by fire. When He reminded me of this, I tried to raise my hands to my nose, but there was no response. I was absolutely helpless. I just said "Amen" to

---

[25] Dabney, Elizabeth Juanita. *What It Means to Pray Through*. Bloomington IN: IUniverse, 1945, 2012.

God in my heart. I lifted my head heavenward and submitted to Him for His will to be done." [26]

As we plan out our campaign to go up a little higher in our walk with the Lord, we should expect His glory to manifest. It may not be in the same way as Mother Dabney. However, He will show Himself, because He said, "If you seek Me, you will find Me, when you search for Me with all your heart" (Jeremiah 29:13).

ACCLIMATIZE – SET YOUR ENVIRONMENT

For climbers, this is adjusting to the climate as you ascend a mountain. The higher you climb, the less oxygen there is. Your body uses oxygen to feed your muscles; the harder you work, the more it needs. Higher altitudes can cause shortness of breath, headaches, and dizziness. Train to be as fit as possible and carefully plan your own acclimatization process to suit your own expedition. [27]

The same goes for your spiritual consecration. Prepare the environment around you to focus on God without distractions. Jesus went away to pray. I cannot reiterate that enough. Find a place absent from the noise of everyday life. Mother Dabney prayed in the church daily. You can create a space or find a place to retreat to. At our church in the Bay area, we would schedule weekends called Encounters. This was a time set aside just to empty ourselves of habits and hang ups, and confront the issues that may have caused us to make detours away from God. The setting was a rustic camp with simple cabins, a community

---

[26] Ibid, 25
[27] Barr

meeting space with a kitchen, manicured grounds, hiking trails and the gorgeous scenery of the majestic Redwood trees in the Santa Cruz mountains. It was the ideal spot to get away to deal with yourself and hear from God. It was two days filled with prayer, praise and worship, applicable Bible teachings and allowing the Holy Spirit to move in our lives in a supernatural way.

If you drove up a little higher past the cabins, you could visit Prayer Mountain. This camp was established to parallel the world-famous Prayer Mountain in Osanri, Kyonggi Province, Korea, founded by Pastor David Yonggi Cho. Our peace-filled camp has small one-room prayer cabins set up similar to the one-room addition the woman built for the prophet Elijah. Each structure is carpeted with a cot or with space for a sleeping bag and a lamp for reading the Bible. Set in God's natural beauty, the camp has walking trails and meeting spaces for large retreats.

TRAVEL LIGHT – CLEAR YOUR MIND

TRAVEL LIGHT

As a mountain climber, you have to be selective about what to pack. Only take what you need to survive. The type of mountain you are climbing determines the type of gear you should be packing: rope, harness, ice axe, clothing for warm or cold conditions, food and water. Any extra, unnecessary weight makes it that much harder to climb. Think breathing through a straw while climbing five flights of stairs. Keeping the weight down can make all the difference.[28]

It's just as important for your environment or climate to be conducive to hear from God. Once you get past the random, inconsequential thoughts – like your grocery list, what you are going to cook for dinner, or why you're even doing this thing; is it really necessary – you can finally hear His still small voice. You might even hear Him say, "Thank you for coming. I've been waiting for you."

Traveling light means clarity, clearing your mind so you can be in the moment. Pastor Wayne Cordeiro emphasized when Bible journaling to have two notebooks, your journal to write down what you hear from scripture and a notebook to jot down those random thoughts like that grocery list, reminders to pick up dry cleaning, set your alarm to walk the dog, anything that pops up as a distraction from your focused time. It is amazing how our minds work. As your journaling routine develops, as you train your mind just as a climber trains their body, the random thoughts become quieter, and less frequent.

Clear your mind

I found the best way to clear your mind is to be cautious about what you expose your mind to. For instance, watching movies and TV Series that are not edifying to your spirit can detract from your time with the Lord, especially if they contain offensive language, sex scenes, and violence. Even some comedies can be outlandish. And don't get me started on reality shows – if you are in consecration, stay away from the

---

[28] Barr

ratchetness! Listening to the cattiness and frustrations in those interactions will only extend the time it takes to quiet your mind and spirit. I know, some of us can get real involved and have real opinions and open communication with the TV screen or portable device while watching.

Climbing higher in your walk with the Lord will take some sacrifice on your part from the things that give pleasure. Regardless of the feel-good-moment, those times can weigh on you. Take off the heaviness. It could also be unintentional, like scrolling through your socials as well as the many images we see of real life. Even the news. All that comes with subliminal messages, usually aimed at causing fear or anxiety. It is not like we don't want to be uninformed of what is happening in the world in some sort of Christian-ese bubble. But it is about knowing what God deems necessary for us to see and care about. He said we are to be in the world and not of the world (John 17:14). We are in the world because that is where we physically live and breathe, and also not of the world because the world does not dictate who we are.

WATCH OUT FOR WEATHER: KNOW THE CLIMATE

WEATHER

Barr's article states, "Bad weather is the biggest single obstacle between success and failure in any climbing expedition."[29] A climber must rely on a weather window, a short period of a few days that allows for ascent and descent before the weather worsens. You have to be prepared to make smart

---

[29] Barr

decisions and be willing to turn back if the weather becomes unfavorable.[30]

We serve a supernatural God whose Kingdom is not of this three-dimensional realm – He is in the fourth dimension. How else did Jesus walk on water, heal the sick, raise the dead, calm raging seas and drive out demons? Knowing the spiritual climate is tapping into that realm and allowing the Holy Spirit to guide you.

This reminds me of a funny story. My sister, Darline, and I had been out together most of the day. Her three children were tweenagers, and we had left them home alone. When we got back to her house, as she walked in the front door, me trailing behind her, she stopped, looked around, and said to her children, "Y'all been fighting."

It was a statement. Not a question.

They all looked at each other and began talking at once to explain and tell-on each other. All I could do was laugh and I still laugh about it today. She knew something was off in her house. And just like she knew the climate of her home was different, we have the capacity in the spirit to know the climate of our environment, so that we can then change the atmosphere.

Darline knew her home, and what the climate or atmosphere should be that brings peace. We need to pay attention to the atmosphere and what is happening around us. Weather is something we cannot control and can sometimes be challenging to predict as the wind shifts.

---

[30] Ibid

The timing of your pursuit will need to incorporate wisdom and discernment. And your best source for wisdom is to follow the leading of the Holy Spirit. Being led by the Spirit requires listening with spiritual ears, Jesus said, "He that hath ears to hear, let him hear what the Spirit is saying to the churches" (Revelation 2:17). Being able to hear in the Spirit is literally getting quiet before the Lord in meditation. David said in Psalms 119:15, *"I will meditate in thy precepts, and have respect unto thy ways"* (KJV).

When we first moved to Las Vegas, I did some research on the history of the city and how it was founded. I wanted to know because we had decided to put a stake in the ground, root ourselves here and we would need to know what we were up against spiritually. I was also curious to know the spiritual climate within the church body. Was it revival, renewal, spiritual warfare, healing, or evangelistic? I took the time to become aware of our new environment, and our new atmosphere.[31]

GET DOWN ALIVE – A POSTURE OF HUMILITY

The heart of the prudent acquires knowledge, And the ear of the wise seeks knowledge. A man's gifts makes room for him, and brings him before great men (Proverbs 18:15-16 NKJV).

"Getting to the top is optional, getting down is mandatory. A classic high-altitude mistake among mountaineers is succumbing

---

[31] I discovered that Nevada was a state that gave writs of divorce within six weeks. A spouse who wanted divorce could come stay here for six weeks and file for divorce. There are over 600 churches in Clark county alone. This led me to believe that history has a spiritual effect indicating why there resides a spirit of division.

to summit fever – you take too long to reach the top and use all your oxygen in the process, thus you don't have enough to safely descend." This wisdom comes from Ed Visteurs, the only American to have climbed all fourteen of the world's 8,000m peaks.[32]

Once you reach that pinnacle moment of His presence, it can be overwhelming. The view at such an altitude is breathtaking, and can literally take your breath away. (Remember the account from Mother Dabney.) While your gifts will make room for you, it's your character that will sustain you. You can climb strictly on talent, but without a proper foundation of knowledge and wisdom, you can destroy all that you have gained simply from pride. As your talents bring you before great men, you can ruin those opportunities with an unbecoming attitude of arrogance.

Coming down from the mountain, you should assume a posture of humility and gratitude. You just successfully reached the peak or summit of that mountain you have been rigorously preparing for. However, the steps down need to be more cautious than going up. Because of the victory you just accomplished, your judgment could potentially be clouded by giving yourself all the praise.

Think of how the disciples wanted to build three altars for Jesus, Moses, and Elijah while on the mountaintop with Jesus. In their flesh, they wanted to remain in that high place. It was a moment of being privy to this transforming experience and hearing God's voice declare who Jesus is. They immediately thought they could contribute to the supernatural act that Jesus

---

[32] Barr

graciously allowed them to witness: that was an act of presumption stemming from pride.

When the Holy Spirit works through us in ministry, it is Him doing the work on behalf of the Father. We are just vessels. What if the basketball itself celebrated that it won the NBA championship, not Lebron James who used it to score the winning shot?

That's us trying to take credit for the move of God in our lives to bless others. God said He hates a proud look. So come down from your mountaintop experience with humility and gratefulness. Be graciously thankful you got to be used by God and had those experiences.

It is not in your strength that you've done anything. It's His. That basketball is a tool those players use to play their game.

Think of a car. The driver has to take care of it in order to get the best use out of it. He has to make sure the engine is tuned up, do consistent oil changes, properly fill it with fluids, and give it a full tank of gas. And that is how God takes care of us. He supplies all of our needs and works things out for our good, so we can be a blessing to others through Him.

Going higher in your walk with the Lord is a discipline you must prepare for. The climb is not about you and your victory: it is about your growth and obedience to Him.

To sum up the spiritual techniques for this journey up your mountain:

Plan your consecration by preparing a place and set time to seek the Lord.

Set your environment by preparing the environment around you to focus on God without distractions.

Clear your mind by being in the moment and cautious about what you expose your mind to.

Know the climate by tapping into the spiritual realm and let the Holy Spirit guide you – basically read the room.

Finally have a posture of humility by being humble. Your judgment could potentially be clouded by the ego of your accomplishment.

Chapter 10
Rough Road Ahead

Under Construction

In a vacant lot across the street from my backyard, a local construction company is preparing to build several single-family homes. While a lot of people might complain about having a construction site so close to their home, I'll be honest: it's been therapeutic watching the construction equipment come in and do their thing.

Several months earlier, I had noticed a tree on the corner of this lot. Over time, I witnessed a whole ecosystem of critters scavenging in and out from this tree. I saw a precious bunny and some desert squirrels just living and scurrying throughout the day. I even noticed a coyote one night as I was pulling out of my security gate and my headlights reflected off of his eyes. I'll admit that part kind of freaked me out.

And then the construction began.

First, the dump trucks came in and dropped loads of rock to prepare a path for the other equipment. I literally watched a bulldozer level that corner tree. What was previously a home for wildlife was now in preparation mode to be a home for people. Then I observed an earth-moving machine called a wheel tractor scraper. It picks up excess dirt as it flattens and levels out the soil surface.

Watching and hearing all this powerful machinery excavating the earth got me thinking of just how similar this construction site is to our spiritual lives.

Whether the process is laying down or excavating, a firm, level foundation is important as you endeavor to build upon it.

Using the Bible as a basis for our foundation is sound doctrine *we c*an build on. The challenge is that our belief systems are often skewed and biased due to our life experiences, cultural influences, and even secular educational theories. We will need to scrape away our old thought patterns, like me watching the excavation equipment tear down the existing foundation to smoothen and level out the ground to construct a new foundation.

And do not be conformed to this world, but be transformed by the renewing of your mind, so that you may prove what the will of God is, that which is good and acceptable and perfect (Romans 12:2 NASB).

As we allow our minds and belief systems to be transformed by God's Word, this enables our foundation to be level, stable, and strong enough to hold up the pillars and beams of our faith. With a firm and sturdy foundation, we can withstand the storms of lies and earthquakes of deceit, the enemy will dispatch. It helps us as Christians to engage in the infallible Truths of the Scripture to understand true authority, and to interpret the Bible in this way.

Being brought up as a Christian, the Bible has always been and will always be a moral compass for my life and all the decisions I make. Using the Scripture during the trying times of my life and especially the pandemic, it has been enlightening and comforting to hear "Thus says the Lord ..."

As the excavation process continues, we are now able to erect new thoughts and apply Kingdom perspectives to those tough situations that arise throughout our journey. Our minds are being renewed in the same fashion as the excess dirt – the unnecessary stuff that has accumulated in our lives – is being scooped up. That also permits us to smooth out the bumps and fill in the cracks as our position in Christ is made secure. In this sense, God is like the wheel tractor scraper.

GRIEF – A ROUGH ROAD TO TRAVEL

My mother and I recently watched an episode of the newly revamped series, *Fantasy Island*. In this reboot, the island is overseen by the niece of the previous host character Mr. Roake. In this particular episode, the show touched on the Mexican or Spanish cultural holiday, the Day of the Dead, *Día de Muertos,* or *Día de los Muertos*. This holiday is a celebration of a brief reunion to welcome the deceased souls of their family members.

In the episode, the island would allow the loved one to actually show up in person for the sake of closure. As we were watching this episode, my mom and I discussed how, there is no way this visitation could be actualized. People would never move on; they would live their lives counting down the days in hopes that their loved ones would appear to them, even if only for one day.

What makes this road of life challenging is having to experience the rough patches: the coarse, uneven rocky path that slows progress, even when there is nothing you can do about it. All you can do is endure it. A particularly rough road to travel is the one of devastation of losing a loved one or close friend and the shock and grief associated with it. There is nothing you can do!

The rough road of grief is a journey we will all eventually have to experience. However, we have the comfort of the

Holy Spirit to help carry us through. If grief is the rough road, then the Holy Spirit acts as the SUV that aids us in maneuvering the bumps, dips, and rocks of this unruly road. We will feel the bumps and agitation of the ride; yet we are comforted by God's Spirit that assures us that He is near, that He loves us, and He is holding us through this. Even though it may not seem like we can handle it, we truly can with God by our side.

In these past few years, we know people who have lost loved ones. We too lost loved ones, we lost friends. But, even in that God's peace surpasses all understanding. Sometimes you don't even realize just how you got through it. I was thinking about my friend LaTanya and how much I loved her and every time I try and grieve for her, it's almost like I can hear her voice, telling me, "Eileen, I'm ok, it's ok."

I feel almost guilty because I feel like I didn't cry enough, and I should be sad. But then the Holy Spirit reminds of who she was in my life and what she represented. We did some amazing things together in ministry. And it wasn't for nothing, we laughed together, cried together, prayed together; she was just an amazing woman of God and a great friend.

I miss her, miss her, miss her, miss her!

For one thing I would have loved to have heard what she would have thought about all this (pandemic), with her quick wit because she was so funny, and would have made us laugh at something.

But even then, while missing her, there was a peace that I walked out of that surpassed all understanding. I could have been extremely distraught because she collapsed in my house and the enemy tried to haunt me with that thought, but again I heard her voice say, "Eileen, I'm ok, it's ok."

I thank God for that.

A pilot on an airplane says to the passengers, "We are going to be experiencing some turbulence. Please sit and make sure your seatbelts are securely fastened." And if the flight is extremely jarring, the pilot tells the flight attendants to stop all aisle service and stabilize themselves. When traveling a rough road your stance is protection – protecting our heart and mind, protecting all our vital places. The enemy tries to use our vulnerabilities against us.

We remember how we are told to put on the full armor of God in Ephesian 6, so we can stand firm against the schemes of the Devil.

Marriage Journey

A marriage too can develop rough patches due to the storms it weathers. I never expected my Journey In Between would also include the space between a happy and unhappy marriage. This is a moment I truly struggled to navigate, mainly because it wasn't just my own thoughts and emotions involved. This included a whole other person.

However, in the eyes of God, we are one. It was like my husband and I were in the garden all over again, and the voice of the Lord came walking through, asking us "Where are you, Derrick and Eileen?" We were somewhere hiding from Him and covering ourselves with the fake masks of a happy marriage, trying to figure it out on our own, separately, and individually. Not together, not as one anymore.

In James Cameron's blockbuster movie *Avatar*, when the indigenous Na'vi people expressed "I see you," they meant "I see into you, I see your heart, I read you," and "I am in this with you."[33] We made mistakes in our relationship not making a conscious effort to "see" one another.

I will take ownership of the fact that I was so inundated with my own hurt, pain, and rejection while trying to find myself, that I neglected my marriage. I had thought that after going through our initial struggles in our early years of marriage, and then applying what we learned from those experiences going forward, that we would always be able to communicate. I took for granted my husband's position, thoughts, and generosity toward me.

When he shared with me his feelings and state of mind after twenty-seven-years of marriage, I was not prepared to hear it. I knew he had some disappointments in certain decisions I made but I did not know they bothered him to the extent of making him unhappy and exhausted from carrying us – me, in particular.

As I stated in a previous chapter, we were both coming to grips with the loss of his dear father and the devastation of losing our friend, LaTanya, within a month of each other. Plus, we were carrying the deep concern for our youngest child enduring back surgery to remove a benign tumor. And all of this during the uncertainty of the COVID-19 Pandemic.

We sought marriage counsel, which was extremely helpful and allowed us both to share and open up to each other without judgment. We both were dealing with so much and instead of

---

[33] Avatar, directed by James Cameron (20th Century Fox 2009).

leaning into each other, we escaped into our own selves. Communication is critical to having a good marriage, and it must be intentional and consistent to have a great one. It is essential to define and apply love and respect as Paul states:

Nevertheless let each one of you in particular so love his own wife as himself, and let the wife see that she respects her husband (Ephesians 5:33 NKJV, emphasis added).

We actually prepared to become more open and intimate with each other. We applied the suggestion of our marriage counselor to incorporate a weekly date night, whether we went out or stayed home. And actually prepared topics to discuss, to dive deeper into our conversations. We both know we'd have to work at this and not take our marriage or one another for granted.

Basically, we are still a work-in-progress, although it's far better.

I also think about my dear friends who have unexpectedly lost their husbands in recent years and how their worlds were turned upside down in a moment. I reflect on those beautiful women, and I will continue to lift them up to the Lord as they navigate their own in between space.

I pray to the Father, "Help me not to take for granted the husband You have blessed me with. Help us to navigate the rough patches with You. Help us to show empathy and demonstrate unconditional love and compassion for each other."

ROUGH ROAD OF REJECTION

To be rejected means not given approval or acceptance. We desire to be accepted. God said in Genesis, "It is not good for man to be alone." We are literally wired to yearn for community and to be a part of a collective. Remember that feeling when you were picked to be on the team on the playground, or in an elite group? It is such a great feeling of belonging and approval by your peers or someone in authority whom you respect.

However, it is that opposite feeling of "rejection" that can be devastating to a child, or even as adults now. (How we draw in social media followers can be the teacher in that lesson.)

I know I have mentioned the church job I lost many times and you must be tired of hearing it. But, to be honest with you, it keeps cropping up whenever I think of my losses. So let me give a full account of what took place so that it might shed some light on the root problem.

In early 2018, our church went through a major ministry transition with a new pastor, new staff, even a new church name. I was on staff during this transition, and while completely caught off-guard by this news of change, was eager to be part of this new team. The conversion was to be complete in about a three-month period. But I was soon told that when the conversion was complete, my services would no longer be needed. I would therefore be released from my full-time staff position, after serving there for eleven years.

Immediately, Proverbs 3:12 came into my mind, "Hope deferred makes the heart sick." I knew I could not finish out the duration of those three months, because naturally, I would try to convince the new administration that I belonged there. I felt like I would have been a blessing to the new ministry and would have fit right in. I felt abandoned by the old staff that were retained because I felt they didn't speak up or vouch for me. I quickly realized everyone at that time was hoping to be picked. I questioned why God would do that. And I knew for sure that the new incoming ministry had missed Him on this one.

I was heartbroken and wondered if I had really heard from God regarding His call on my life. I took on another position with a non-profit professional women's organization. But because I was still grieving for my previous job, I was not prepared to move forward, and I lost that job.

Shortly after that, we made the decision to move to Las Vegas.

All at once, I had no family near me, no church home, no close friends, or a job. The rejection piled on when I kept receiving job reject emails. I felt displaced, depressed, and rejected. While walking this bumpy road of rejection, I had to turn introspective to see *my* faults. I needed to assess how and why the grief of losing my jobs affected me so much.

I came to realize that God knows what is best for me, and that He must be preparing me for something good. Meanwhile, I had to confront my feelings of displacement, depression, and rejection. It took almost two years for the healing of my heart because I could feel the wound every time that area was touched upon.

THE EXCAVATION

Watching the construction equipment across my backyard excavate the dirt, reminds me of what God has done and is still doing for me, as this vessel is always subject to remolding by the Potter. God says in Isaiah 43, He is doing a new thing, and to do this new thing, He has to prepare the way and remove the old. He says for us not to remember the former things or consider the things of old.

For me, I had to first understand and then release what had happened to me especially my feelings of betrayal and rejection. I blamed God and I blamed others. I had to forgive those whom I felt had hurt me and caused me pain. I had to forgive myself for being stuck in that place, and I even had to forgive myself for the blame I placed on God.

Excavation is the process of moving earth, rock, and other materials with special equipment. It also involves assessing the type of soil and clearing the site of unwanted bushes, weeds, and débris. As the old topsoil is removed, the excavation equipment exposes the next layer of earth, creating a fresh space to begin laying down the new foundation to build upon.

Interestingly, that is what God is doing for us. He removes the old topsoil – our old ways of thinking and feelings harbored – so He can prepare a way to begin something new that will spring forth.

I came across an interesting article in *Drilling and Excavation Blog*, which outlines Five Steps of Excavation: Rough Staking, Clearing, Excavation, Rough Grading, and Erosion Control.[34]

---

[34] Lassiter Excavating, "The Five Steps of Excavation," Drilling and Excavation Blog, February 21, 2018 accessed October 16, 2021 https://lassiterexcavating.com/blog/the-five-steps-of-excavation/

Could it be a coincidence that these five steps line up with the Word of God? Let's look at Isaiah 40:3-5 (NIV).

Step 1. Rough Staking - *A voice of one calling*:
"*In the wilderness prepare
   the way for the* LORD ... (Isaiah 40:3ª)

This is the process in which God calls forth His plans and begins to map out a space to begin something new in our lives. He removes our previous roles (trees), positions (bushes) and débris (issues) that would hinder our "next." He does not want us in the same place, doing the same things we have always done.

The step of rough staking is planting the sticks with the colored flags on top in the ground of a new construction site. It is an illustration of how God lays out the stakes in accordance with the design of what He is going to build in us. We cannot see the layout. We just feel the pain of the uprooting and pruning as our precious vocation (way of life) is being stripped from us.

Step 2. Clearing - *Make straight in the desert, a highway for our God* (Isaiah 40:3ᵇ).

Remember that ecosystem being swiped away by the bulldozer? This is that process, the clearing of all vegetation or tree roots. Make straight in the wilderness is clearing out a pathway for God to move within us.

The wilderness can become a wasteland, a desert, a wild and untamed place. This is the clearing of the deep root systems and old thought processes that can hinder the new movement of God. Just like that ecosystem was a home and way life for many critters, we have ecosystems that we cling to. For instance, we may believe we have reached our pinnacle, our mountaintop, our top-of-our-game moment. And then it comes crumbling down, and we don't understand when God closes that door. He must clear out what was planted and was nourishing us at that time, in order to use fresh soil to seed what can feed and nurture us in this new season.

Step 3. Excavation - *Every valley shall be raised up [exalted] and every mountain and hill made [brought] low* … (Isaiah 40:4ᵃ, emphasis added)

This is the process in which excess dirt is removed using heavy equipment like a bulldozer or backhoe, as well as dump trucks to haul away the fill.

The valley being raised is you coming out of depression and the low places of your thinking because now you have a better view. That is the plus side of excavation.

The downside is… this part hurts like hell – the scraping, the digging, the pounding, the leveling – as all your successes are made low. The mountains you climbed and the hills you conquered are now past tense. Your accomplishments are no longer celebrated in the present and the memorial mounds of those triumphs are being hauled away. Remember He is doing a new thing; you cannot put new wine in old wine skins. It's just like an Oscar winning actor will always be an Oscar winner, but they don't play that same character in every new movie. They must move on and prepare for the next role.

Step 4. Rough-Grading - *The rough ground shall become level, the rugged places plain [The crooked places shall be made straight and the rough places smooth]* (Isaiah 40:4, emphasis added).

This fourth step is where some of the dirt which was removed during excavation can be re-used to back-fill around the home to establish the right height toward the curb, for drainage purposes. The richer topsoil that was removed can now be added to fill in for growth like grass and shrubbery.

This is the process where all things become level and you get to begin again. Not so much a starting over from scratch, but a restart with more experiences and wisdom in your arsenal. You've learned from previous experiences, and you get a chance to begin again with a fresh perspective.

Step 5. Erosion Control - *The glory of the LORD shall be revealed, And all people will see it together. For the mouth of the LORD has spoken* (Isaiah 40:5).

Erosion is the detachment of soil, sediment, or rock fragments caused by wind, water, ice and/or gravity. Erosion Control prevents the topsoil from being eroded away.

The glory of the Lord revealed is like a form of erosion control. His presence is a deterrent for the principalities and entities that lurk about trying to creep in and undermine our thoughts about who God says we are. His presence prevents the breakdown of what He is building up in us.

This is the time to acknowledge God for His handiwork and praise Him for His mighty acts, as praising God stops the enemy in his tracks. All mankind, flesh or peoples shall see it together or at the same time, because it will manifest outwardly like fresh sprigs of grass and blooming flowers. Our countenance is uplifted and refreshed. The mouth of the Lord has spoken through the affirmation and application of God's Word in our lives.

A word of caution: traveling this road is extremely uncomfortable, unavoidable, and uncertain. However, being strapped in by the Holy Spirit allows this unbearable ride to be doable. But the benefits of that stripping process are greater than anything we can fathom.

CHAPTER 11
CELEBRATING MILESTONES

A Time to Celebrate

These stones are to be a memorial to the people of Israel forever ... He said to the Israelites, In the future when you descendants ask their parents, 'What do these stones mean?' tell them, Israel crossed the Jordan on dry ground (Joshua 4:7, 21-22 NIV).

What is a milestone? A milestone is a stone by the side of a road that shows the distance (in between) in miles to a specified place.[35] This is the space or time we acknowledge how far we have come, and mark it, or just recognize the distance. Milestones are markers of progress to let you know from where you've been. They signify an action or event marking an observable change or stage in development.

Celebrating milestones is celebrating the fact that you trekked across the plains, were tested in the wilderness, survived the jungle, weathered the desert, encountered the valley, climbed the mountain and tackled the rough road. Let's celebrate these milestones. And let's apply the lessons learned from those experiences.

We learned that just as there is a time for everything under heaven, our in between moments are divinely purposed. These moments are essential pauses as we transition from one phase of our lives to the next.

As we trekked across the plains, we recognized God as our Navigator and Captain and the Holy Spirit as our Compass. We sensed the presence of our Savior all along the journey. Though

---

[35] (Miriam-Webster)

the plains were uneventful, He encouraged us to keep moving forward and look to the hills.

The test of the wilderness was to trust God no matter what. We were to actually apply the Word of God to life's moments. I literally had to walk in the Spirit to not be deceived by the enemy and fall into my own lusts or emotional swings. The terrain of this barren and desolate wasteland of trials tested my spiritual stamina and my identity in Christ enough to wonder "Am I who God says I am?"

God allowed us to learn who we were through the jungle. He let us know that we had the power and the authority through His Word, to stand firm in those attacks coming at us from all different directions. Jungles don't necessarily always have a path and sometimes you have to swipe out that path using the sword of the Spirit, which is the Word of God.

When we got to the desert, I was in a dry place – in a drought – waiting for the environment to shift and change so that I could be in the fruitful position that God has for me. I wasn't ready to be in this position before: I needed to escape the drought and be buried. Sometimes we think our dreams and visions are dead and in the ground, when in fact they are just waiting to be awakened by a favorable environment and spring forth. I can feel a change and movement happening in my spirit already.

In the valley we encountered grief and sadness and we discovered that this was no place to stay. The valley is a pathway and not a destination. God showed Himself faithful and He was there as the Lily of the Valley, beckoning me into closer relationship with Him as the bridegroom.

The mountain climb was grueling, and it took a time of spiritual preparation. We had to make sure we were ready for the challenge. This was a time of assessment and allowed only taking what was necessary for this journey. I realized that Kingdom living is intentional. No one climbs a mountain by accident. In order to grow in Christ you must put forth the effort through discipline, and the Spirit of the Lord will take it from there.

I learned that confronting the rough road was confronting myself. We have to deal with our pain and issues and discover the root causes in order to be free enough to get to our next. I needed to let go even of meaningful things that would not serve me on my next level.

We are yet exploring and navigating new territory but, in the meantime, we need to continue to celebrate how far we have come.

The Old Testament saints would stop and build an altar or make a pile of stones as a memorial to praise and worship God for what He had brought them through. This is the time of worship unto the Lord. Like the old song says, "As I look back over my life and see what I have been through, I can truly say that I've been blessed, I have a testimony."

The memorial of praise and thanksgiving we erect is our time for testimony. In all things let us give thanks for letting Him work all things for our good.

ABOUT THE AUTHOR

Author's Bio

Eileen Deadwiler hails from North Las Vegas, NV, where she lives with her husband Derrick and a lovable boxer/pit named Dexter. She is the mother of four young adult children and currently has one son-in-love. Her authorship began when she wrote the book she sought to read, *The Journey in Between: Navigating the Terrain in Between Life's Moments*. At an age when many people are settling into who they have become, Eileen at fifty was starting over in a new state, settling into a new home, crossing a threshold in her relationship with her husband as empty nesters, and not knowing what was next for her. So, she began to write.

During her in between moment, she launched a podcast, earned a Graduate Certificate in Christian Theology, and was presented with a proclamation from the City of Las Vegas for her virtual Bible Study during the COVID-19 Pandemic, awarded June 2, 2021, as *Eileen Deadwiler Day*.

INDEX

Abraham, 45

Acts, 33, 46, 50

Acts of God, 48

Angels, 20, 21, 22, 23

Apostle Jude, 39

Apostle Paul, 32, 33, 38, 43

Archon, 40

Armour of God, 38, 43

Barr, Matt, 83

Belt of Truth, 44

Bible, 9, 22, 33, 47, 50, 51, 54, 57, 68, 71, 73, 87, 88, 97, 115

Biblical values, 41

Birth, 2, 3

Black American, 30, 47

Blood of the Lamb, 38

Body of Christ, 47, 51

Bread, 18, 19

Breastplate, 43, 45

Broadnax, LaTanya, 65

Bryant, Kobe, 28

Cameron, James, 101

Chairo, 32, 33

Childhood trauma, 6, 39

Christ's Word, 47

Christian warrior, 44, 51

Chronicles, 51, 52

Church administration, 55

Church of God, 85

Church of Jesus Christ, 49

Consecration, 83, 84, 86, 88

Consequences of sin, 48

Cordeiro, Pastor Wayne, 88

Corinthians, 42, 45, 47, 57

Covid-19, 51, 101, 115

Index

Dabney, Mother Elizabeth Juanita, 85

Deadwiler, Eileen, 70, 115

Death, 2, 24, 25, 29, 32, 44, 48, 67, 85

    Certain, 48
    Resurrection, 79
    Shadow, 66

Demonic powers, 41

Demonic spirits, 41

Depression, 29, 34, 65, 67, 71, 75, 104, 107

Deuteronomy, 19, 22

Día de Muertos, 98

Disciples, 9, 72, 79, 80, 92

Discipline, 82, 83, 93, 114

Divine punishment, 6

Divinely appointed, 4, 5, 59

Dollar, Creflo, 67

Ecclesiastes, 2, 3, 5, 6

Egyptians, 23

Encounters, 86

Enemy, 30, 34, 38, 39, 42, 43, 45, 47, 48, 49, 50, 52, 85, 97, 100, 108, 113

    Chaos, 46
    Darts, 35
    Influence, 41
    Jesus, 21, 25
    Temptation, 18

Enemy of our souls, 17, 29, 39

Ephesians, 29, 34, 38, 40, 43, 57, 100, 102

Evil, 20, 41, 43, 47

Evil powers of darkness, 41

Excavation, 105, 107

Fantasy Island, 98

Five landscapes

    The desert, 2, 23, 54, 55, 58, 59, 60, 106, 112, 113

    The jungle, 2, 28, 34, 38, 51, 112, 113

    The mountaintop, 2, 92

    The plains, 2, 10, 12, 13, 112, 113

Index

The valley, 2, 63, 64, 65, 66, 67, 70, 71, 74, 75, 76, 112, 113

Flesh and blood, 38, 40

Floyd, George, 47

Galatians, 17

Gates of Hell, 43

Genesis, 4, 17, 18, 20, 23, 47, 67, 103

God
    Control, 5
    In the beginning, 4, 67
    Integrity, 48
    Navigator, 9
    Our past, 6
    Peace, 32
    Praise, 25
    Provider, 16
    Purpose, 5
    Safety, 22
    the Father, 8

God's Divinity, 4

God's favor, 33

God's grace, 33

God's image, 20

God's plan, 70, 76

God's righteous laws, 41

God's Word, 10, 18, 42, 47, 97, 108

Goldblum, Jeff, 21

Gospel, 41, 43, 45, 46

Greed, 25

Grieson, Mike, 8

Guerrilla tactics, 39

Guerrilla warfare, 39, 51

Heavenly realm, 41

Hebrews, 25, 26, 50, 83

High level leaders, 41

High Priest, 26

His glory, 44, 86

His goodness, 25, 57

Holy Spirit, 67, 82, 87, 93, 99, 108
    Acts, 50
    Advocate, 9
    Guide, 9, 13, 90, 112
    Mathew, 18
    Navigator, 10
    Truth, 9
    Wisdom, 90

Index

Humility, 51, 92, 93

Illness, 48

Isaiah, 6, 13, 45, 47, 51, 55, 60, 66, 75, 105, 106, 107, 108

Israelites, 22, 112

Jeremiah, 2, 76, 86

Jerusalem, 73

Jesus

  The Son, 8
Jesus as Savior, 43

Jesus Christ, 34, 49, 51

Jesus is Lord, 49

John, 16, 48, 73, 74, 89

John's Gospel, 9

Journey In Between, 1, 12, 100

Jude, 39

Jurassic Park, 21

Kingdom, 9, 23, 24, 30, 31, 82, 90, 97, 114

  Of God, 31
Lily of the Valley, 69, 71, 72, 76, 113

Lust, 16, 17, 20, 21, 42

Mankind, 19

Manna, 23

Mark, 24, 79

Marriage, 44, 74, 100, 101, 102

Mathew, 17, 18, 19, 20, 22, 23, 25, 44, 49, 79

McNab, Neil, 83

Moral values, 41

Mother Dabney, 86, 92

Mountaineer Mindset, 78

Navigator, 8, 9, 10, 17, 112

Nehemiah, 59, 75

New Testament, 23

NKJV, 6, 9, 16, 17, 19, 20, 23, 24, 25, 26, 45, 50, 57, 58, 74, 91, 102

Old Testament, 23, 114

Pandemic, 4, 9, 28, 32, 51, 66, 68, 97, 99, 101, 115

Perfection of Christ, 45

Perkins, Andy, 83

Peter, 30, 49, 79, 80

Index

Philippians, 32, 50

Phillips, Dr. Anita, 32

Pillars of Christianity, 49

Plague, 23

Powers, 40

Prayer, 31, 33, 38, 43, 51, 52, 82, 84, 85, 87

Prayer Mountain, 87

Pride of life, 16, 17, 23, 25

Principality, 40

Procreation, 44

Prophet Elijah, 87

Proverbs, 8, 67, 91, 103

Psalm, 14, 21, 51, 57, 62, 75, 76, 91

Racism, 73

Reproduction rights, 44

Resurrection, 44, 79

Revelation, 58, 75, 91

Rhema word, 50

Righteousness, 34, 43, 45, 47, 49

Rock of the Word, 49

Romans, 4, 5, 10, 31, 36, 48, 49, 76, 97

Ruach, 22

Rulers of the darkness, 41

Saints, 43, 51, 52, 114

Salvation, 25, 43, 48, 49, 71

Samaria, 46, 72, 73

Satan, 18, 25, 40, 41, 42, 85

Scripture, 5, 6, 13, 17, 19, 21, 24, 30, 32, 45, 47, 49, 50, 54, 55, 56, 82, 84, 88, 97

Selah, 22

Serenity, 46

Sexism, 73

Shield of faith, 43, 46, 47, 48

Social media, 16, 84, 103

Solomon, 6

Son of God, 18, 19, 20, 24, 49

Song of Solomon, 71

Sonship, 21

Index

Soul, body, and spirit, 19

Spirit filled life, 43

Spirit of God, 17

Spirit of Truth, 9

Spiritual leaders, 29

Spiritual mountains, 82

Spiritual wickedness, 41

Spurgeon, Charles, 71

Subliminal messages, 89

Supplication, 31, 33, 43, 51

Surviving in the Desert, 58

Sword of the Spirit, 36, 43, 49, 50, 113

Sychar, 72

Temptation, 16, 18, 19, 22, 25

The Journey in Between, 3, 70, 115

The Rose and the Lily, 71

Times of uncertainty, 29

Timothy, 49, 51

Transition points, 2

Triune God, 8

Truth
    Facts vs., 9
    Gospel, 42

Ukraine and Russia War, 32

Ultimate sacrifice, 24, 75

Visteurs, Ed, 91

Wicked one, 46

Wilderness, 13, 16, 17, 20, 28, 50, 55, 59, 106, 112, 113

Wilds of the Devil., 39

Will of God, 18, 31, 97

Word of God, 2, 5, 10, 18, 31, 35, 38, 43, 47, 48, 49, 50, 51, 75, 106, 113

Worship, 23, 41, 60, 63, 66, 68, 73, 74, 75, 76, 85, 87, 114

Zschech, Darlene, 76

APPENDIX

Appendix A

Ecclesiastes 3: 1-

(By no means are these exhaustive definitions, but hopefully will help with comprehension):

A time to give birth and a time to die;

This verse refers to birth, to be born, or to become new. It can relate to a new season in life, a new start, or a new beginning. Examples could be starting a family, birthing a dream, a business, or maybe a new project.

When something dies, its life has ceased. It means to end or to let go. The cycle is over, or the life of a thing is finished, it's complete. Examples could be the end of your life, or a loved one, or letting go of a relationship or career.

A time to plant and a time to uproot what is planted.

Planting is preparing for a future harvest. It implies preparation of life, to prepare for growth. You take the time to nourish, to water, to invest in what is planted. I heard someone say, just because something is buried doesn't mean it is dead, it's just planted.

To uproot in another translation is pluck up, or to break off the vine. This is a time to reap the harvest for it is ripe (ready). This is a time to receive what you have gained from your investment. This could represent knowledge, a college degree, experience, or revenue. It can also mean a time to remove that which is no longer working for you in your current season.

A time to kill and a time to heal;

To kill is to intentionally end the life of someone or something. You purposely stop the growth and end on purpose. An example would be to kill an idea or kill the marriage contract; divorce.

To heal means to restore back to its original condition, or better. Another definition is to restore health.

To fix what is broken: your heart, a relationship, an illness.

A time to tear down and a time to build up.

When something is torn down, you break down, shatter or sever something that is moving upward or growing. This could mean breaking down whatever is ascending. Tear down someone's confidence and break their stride. Or a builder tearing down a wall because it's crooked.

To build up, means to add to, expand, or top off. You can build up by encouragement, expressing uplifting words of praise, like building up a person's confidence.

A time to weep and a time to laugh;

A time to weep means to cry, to shed tears, to allow overflow of sorrowful or sad emotions. Weeping implies mourning over something that has ended, gone or died. But also remember that tears can cleanse and can be necessary.

To laugh means to have joy. It's a natural reaction to something funny, to feel good, to be happy, or to be merry. Think puns.

Why did the baker cross the road?

Appendix

Why?

He had muffin else to do.

You see. A time to laugh.

Or groan. Whatever.

A time to mourn and a time to dance.

To mourn means to feel deep sorrow, or even regret, for the loss or disappearance of someone or something, including moments of grief.

To dance means to celebrate, to move in a joyful way.

A time to throw stones and a time to gather stones;

Stones can represent judgment, memorials, or altars. To cast away (or throw) means to push away, get rid of, trash it, throw away or reject.

Gathering stones means bringing together, to huddle, or to assemble.

A time to embrace and a time to shun embracing.

To embrace means to bring in, to accept, to hold dear, or to cherish.

To shun or refrain from embracing, means to push away or to reject.

A time to search and a time to give up as lost;

To search means to seek out to add to or discover. To multiply, to win, to be found, maybe even revenue.

To give up as lost or lose means to subtract from, to not win, to be lost or to be depleted.

A time to keep and a time to throw away.

Time to keep means to hold on, to be held, or to save.

Time to throw away means to let go intentionally or deliberately.

A time to tear apart and a time to sew together;

To tear apart means to rip or split.

To sew implies to mend, to make whole.

A time to be silent and a time to speak.

To be silent suggests being quiet, not speaking, or doing nothing.

To speak indicates to say something, vocal expression, do something, or act.

A time to love and a time to hate;

To love infers to cherish, embrace, care, show empathy or sacrifice for.

To hate means to abhor, not like, despise, or enmity.

A time for war and a time for peace.

Time for war entails a fight, violence against opposition, or physical disagreement.

Time for peace denotes agreement, on the same page, calmness, and serenity.

Appendix B – Warfare in the Jungle

This tactic and strategy were proven by Jesus because the full armor of God is Jesus:

Truth – John 14:6

Righteousness – Romans 3:22; 1 Corinthians 1: 30

Peace – John 14:27

Faith – Hebrews 12:2

Salvation – Isaiah 12:2

Word made flesh – John 1:1;14